BRITISH RAIL AT WORK:
ScotRail

Colin Boocock

LONDON

IAN ALLAN LTD

Acknowledgements

Producing a book on a current, up-to-date subject presents different challenges compared with a more stable, historical publication. The author is grateful for help and advice, information and material provided by the following friends and colleagues. He hopes he has omitted no-one from the list. The order is alphabetic: John Boyle, Willie Caldwell, Vivian Chadwick, Jim Cornell, Chris Green, Geoff James, Andy Love, Robin Nelson, Tom Noble, George O'Hara and Peter Skelton.

Dedication

This book is dedicated to Mary.

Photographs

All photographs in this book were taken by the author, unless otherwise credited.

Right:
The Forth bridge dominates the background behind No 47.702 *Saint Cuthbert* as it leaves Inverkeithing with the 17.42 from Edinburgh to Kirkcaldy on 10 August 1983. *G. W. Morrison*

First published 1986

ISBN 0 7110 1567 8

Published by Ian Allan Ltd, Shepperton, Surrey; and printed by Ian Allan Printing Ltd at its works at Coombelands in Runnymede, England

Contents

FOREWORD

J. Cornell
General Manager
ScotRail

In 1983 the word 'ScotRail' barely existed. Today it is recognised, nationally and internationally, as the name adopted by the Scottish Region of British Rail to describe and promote itself and its services.

That recognition is no accident. As the text and illustrations of this publication well show, a very great deal has been achieved by ScotRail within a very short timescale. It has been the quite remarkable nature, speed and number of these achievements (and their aggressive promotion) which have made ScotRail the focus of so much public and media interest.

There can be no doubt that this region of British Rail (for which no one five years ago would have predicted a bright future) has been transformed. Defeatism and retreat have been replaced by some of the most positive thinking and direct action within British Rail. The spur has been a determination to survive in quite the most competitive public transport market in the United Kingdom . . . and to succeed in a way none would have thought possible.

I have been privileged to enjoy the excitement of having had a part to play in many parts of what people have described as 'The ScotRail Phenomenon'.

It is a feeling I know I share with my predecessor, Chris Green, and with a great many ScotRail colleagues who worked so very hard and sacrificed so very much to make ScotRail a force to be reckoned with in the market place. It is upon their continuing effort and dedication that ScotRail must depend to maintain and improve a market share which in 1983 was being so tragically lost to growing competition from air and road transport. I am confident that the ScotRail momentum will be sustained and that the future of Scotland's railways will thereby be the more assured.

I therefore welcome the publication of this excellent work by Colin Boocock for the light it sheds on the renaissance of British Rail in Scotland.

Above:
J. Cornell. *BR*

Left:
ScotRail House in Glasgow houses the Region's headquarters staff.

Preface:
'ScotRail the Brave'

'Why is the Scottish Region so often in the forefront of such developments?' Thus ran a recent magazine editorial commenting on British Rail's efforts to improve the travel environment of the railway passenger.

In later pages of this book will be found many examples of BR Scotland's ability to reach and enact business decisions quickly, and to make regular and often substantial improvements to the railway, often without the dramatic expenditure of large sums of money.

As a Region its situation is unique in many ways. Firstly, its territory is simply the whole country of Scotland. Secondly, its balance of traffics puts it predominantly into BR's Provincial sector (to which it contributes around 14% of that sector's fare revenues). Thirdly, its apparent semi-independence is emphasised by its distance from Board headquarters in London. Fourthly, and perhaps most significantly, it was the first Region to adopt a two-tier management structure, eliminating the divisional level from most functions. In this two-tier system the area managers and area maintenance engineers report directly to senior managers at Regional headquarters, in this case at ScotRail House, Glasgow. This shortens the chain of command and gives a better chance for new initiatives to be heard and adopted. It is also more cost-effective.

The Scottish Region has come up with a number of 'firsts' in the 1980s to improve its customer appeal or economy of operation. These are developed at greater length in the chapters and photograph captions which follow, and include:

● The first commercial use of two-wire push-pull control on BR.
● Differential speed limits which benefit InterCity 125s and cut journey times.
● Marginal use of air-conditioned carriages to benefit commuters and meet coach competition.
● The invention of ETHEL to enable the Fort William sleeping cars to keep running.
● Running mixed-brake freight/passenger trains to the far north.
● Implementation of radio-controlled block signalling.
● Trolley snacks in trains not conveying catering cars.
● The first 100mph working of Class 47 locomotives.
● The first application of a Passenger Transport Executive livery to suburban multiple-units.
● The first rebuilt station specifically laid out as an 'open station', at Haymarket.

These and many other initiatives brighten what otherwise might too easily have become a low-maintenance, low-investment, low-quality backwater of the national railway system. BR Scotland has a relatively small stake in InterCity revenue and hence investment, and is a net importer of goods which reflects to an extent in its freight revenue also. It therefore relies heavily on the Provincial sector, and on the Region's excellent relationships with ~cal authorities, for financial support.

Hopefully, on browsing through these pages, readers will gain an impression of a lively, active railway system that gets the best out of its ageing assets, and above all provides value for money.

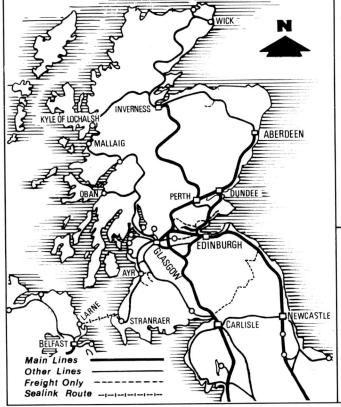

Main Lines ————
Other Lines ————
Freight Only ----------
Sealink Route —·—·—·—·—·—

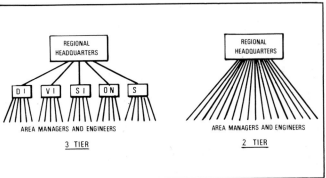

Above:
An example of elegance in diesel traction: No 47.712 *Lady Diana Spencer* prepares to leave Glasgow's Queen Street terminus with the 07.30 push-pull train to Edinburgh on 12 June 1981.

Right:
Threading the timeless scenery of the line to Kyle of Lochalsh in 1973 is Class 25 No 5120 heading a morning down parcels train

alongside Loch Carron.
J. H. Cooper-Smith

Below:
Scotland pioneered the use of two-wire control in push-pull trains on the Edinburgh-Glasgow line. In this view of the 11.30 to Glasgow emerging from the Mound tunnel on 26 April 1983, the locomotive, unmanned, propels the train at the rear.

Above:
The Scottish pioneering streak is evident again in this view of No 37.081 *Loch Long* passing through Taynuilt with an Oban to Edinburgh return excursion in July 1983. The use of an ETHEL train heat generator vehicle (behind the locomotive) enabled an air-conditioned set to be rostered.

Right:
The pleasant front outline of the Glasgow suburban 'blue trains' has already changed since this 1981 picture of two sets at Glasgow Central was taken. These units are now being painted in the livery of Strathclyde Passenger Transport Executive.

Below right:
Strathclyde Transport is the proud logo on the side of an orange-and-black Class 303 electric multiple-unit (EMU) at Glasgow Central on 1 October 1983.

Above:
The Class 107, Derby heavyweight, medium-density diesel multiple-units (DMUs) are unique to Scotland (with the exception of one trailer car on the Buxton branch!). Set No 107.440 leads the 07.52 from Largs to Glasgow Central into Johnstone station on 9 October 1982.

Left:
With its coaches endorsed with the ScotRail legend, the 14.20 from Inverness to Edinburgh approaches Tomatin on 20 July 1984.

Below left:
Clean roof glazing, bold advertising panels, and the bright, terrazzo-tiled concourse floor, combine to place Glasgow Queen Street as one of Britain's brightest terminal stations.

Above:
The new ScotRail identity
includes the livery of main line
trains in Scotland. No 47.711
Greyfriars Bobby and its train are
painted two-tone grey with bold
white-and-blue longitudinal
stripes; the locomotive cabs are
yellow with black window
surrounds. The train is the 20.00
to Edinburgh, photographed on
16 January 1985 at Glasgow
Queen Street.

Left:
The light and cheery interior of
Glasgow Queen Street embraces
Class 101 DMU set No 360 on the
14.38 to Dunblane.

11

1
Premier Line

The Englishman's or Welshman's impression of Glasgow too often comes from the media's unfailing coverage of bad news. Still too many people are not aware that this home of three-quarters of a million ebulliently loyal people is, quite definitely, Britain's finest Victorian city, that it has more public parks than any other British town, is a very fine cultural centre, and that as a tourist centre its proximity to Loch Lomond and the Trossachs makes it an ideal springboard for exploring Scotland's beautiful scenery.

Not surprisingly, therefore, Glasgow is the terminating point of Britain's longest electrified main line: the West Coast main line stretches 401 miles from London Euston to Glasgow Central, and around 90 miles of it are north of the border. The northbound traveller enters Scotland as the train crosses flat farmland north of Carlisle and clatters across the junction with the former Glasgow & South Western Railway at Gretna. For a while the line curves and undulates through pleasant farm country before and after the small town of Lockerbie, the southerner's first sight of a typical Scottish stone townscape. Before long the railway begins to climb in earnest – a longer, tougher climb than that over Shap because the incline to Beattock summit rises to a greater height and continues unbroken. Adhesion conditions here are often the worst on BR's main lines, and even modern Class 87 electric locomotives can 'lose their feet' on particularly 'driech' days.

These southern uplands are softer in profile than the Grampians or other mountain ranges further north in Scotland, but they provide the traveller with a pleasant introduction to Scottish scenery. Even here the population is predominantly sheep.

Dropping beyond the Abington loops, this former Caledonian main line takes a series of wide sweeps through barren valleys, round some very long continuous curves through which InterCity trains hurtle at high cant-deficiency speeds. But soon the Lanarkshire landscape appears with the now familiar signs of former industries and communities affected by reduced employment. Passing the great Ravenscraig steelworks, the main line drops down heading west through Motherwell, crosses the Clyde valley just beyond Uddingston, glimpses an orange electric train at Newton and enters Glasgow city to pass rapidly through Cambuslang, past Rutherglen's new suburban station and the modern carriage depot at Polmadie, past the Freightliner depot at Gushetfaulds, and swings to the north again on slab track through the short tunnels under two main city radial roads. Joined now by other electrified suburban lines, the main line crosses the Clyde again, this time with dignity on a grand Victorian bridge, and ends under the vast glass-panelled overall roof of Glasgow's Central station.

Above:
Dominated by the Scottish uplands, electric locomotive No 86.039 powers at speed through Crawford in April 1979 with a train from Edinburgh and Glasgow to the English Midlands. The rear four coaches (from Edinburgh) were attached to the main train (from Glasgow) at Carstairs.
L. A. Nixon

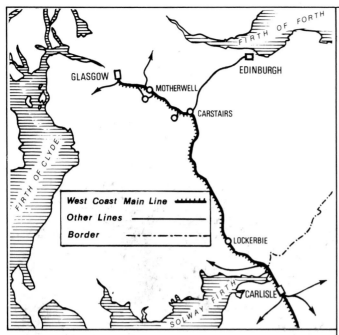

West Coast Main Line ┉┉┉┉
Other Lines ────────
Border ─·─··─··─

The passenger from London alighting at Glasgow Central will usually be greeted by lively music over the station's loudspeaker system, flowers on the platforms, and in summer a uniformed hostess through whom to channel his enquiries. Outside he will find conveniently the orange single-deck bus that links Central with Queen Street station for the railways to the north. For it is an oft-forgotten fact that when a passenger crosses the border at Gretna he is well under the half-way mark on a journey from Euston to Wick!

The West Coast main line entered the 1980s after a period of consolidation following the opening of electrification in 1974. Civil engineering problems relating to the sub-structure of much of the main line in England south of Preston, plus the need to tap business at more stations, had caused the five-hour London to Glasgow timings of 1974 to be short-lived, and by 1982 the 'Royal Scot's' southbound journey time was five hours 28 minutes. The airlines had acquired 80% of the business travel market on the Glasgow-London route. The introduction of Mk 3a locomotive-hauled carriages in 1975 had not had the impact that the InterCity 125s had had on other routes, because they did not herald speed improvements. Also, they relied on Mk 1 catering cars for several more years, and the 'nose cone effect' of a streamlined train to impress the public's visual senses was lacking.

Thus it was that the electric version of the Advanced Passenger Train (APT) was considered to be the answer. It provided the option of a high top speed of at least 125mph, and tilting coaches enabled it to negotiate curves much faster than conventional stock. During its prolonged trials it proved the technical feasibility of tilting and the lower-profile, lightweight body structures. The outer bogies (under the driving cabs) gave excellent riding qualities. The articulation was less successful however, and the technology surrounding operation of the otherwise excellent hydrokinetic brake gave rise to problems. The power-car traction equipment was superb though lessons had to be learned in the design and lubrication of the gearboxes which transferred power from the body-mounted traction motors to the bogies.

The APT-P sets have run hundreds of thousands of miles in proving many component designs and their developments. This experience has led to the proposal to produce a push-pull tilting train using APT-style vehicles, each on two bogies, powered by a lightweight Bo-Bo electric locomotive. Currently code-named InterCity 225, this will lift speeds at the end of this decade to bring the Glasgow-London run much closer to a competitive four-hour timing, providing high-quality accommodation at acceptable maintenance costs.

Until then, steps need to be taken to bring timings to a more competitive level. In 1984 the first step was taken to raise the running speeds of certain InterCity Executive trains to 110mph. This was achieved by fitting Class 87s with BR/Brecknell-Willis Highspeed pantographs and by raising the braking rates on the associated Mk 3a stock. It is further planned to increase the acceptable level of cant-deficiency so that trains can run through curves faster, and work is in progress on ironing out locations where curves impose speed restrictions. The speed limit through Crewe, for example, has been raised from 20mph to 80mph as a result of remodelling. Steps such as these should enable Glasgow passengers to have a regularly improving journey time to and from England for many years to come.

Another batch of West Coast main line trains is the Anglo-Scottish group that starts from both Glasgow and Edinburgh and combines at Carstairs to go forward to places such as Manchester, Nottingham, Liverpool, Birmingham and Harwich (Parkestone Quay). From 1982 these have been formed of Mk 2d and 2e stock based at Polmadie (Glasgow) for maintenance, plus a few carriage sets from the Western Region. Destinations are expanding and some have ventured further afield to Bournemouth and Poole and even to Penzance. The latter carries carriages for Aberdeen to produce BR's longest through passenger journey! The 'Clansman' is another well-known long day-time run, entering Scotland at Gretna, turning north at Motherwell and continuing to Stirling, Perth and stations to Inverness.

There have also been developments in the 1980s on overnight passenger trains. In 1982, to combat luxury road coach competition, BR put on the 'Nightrider' trains which, from 1983, included one between Glasgow and Euston via the West Coast route, formed of Mk 2d stock. The most significant move was the replacement of Mk 1 sleeping cars by the new Mk 3a sleepers: a contemporary television advertisement made capital out of the fact that many passengers in these are not immediately aware when their train begins to move, so smooth and quiet are these superb vehicles!

The overnight passenger trains are pathed between flights of freight trains, Freightliners in particular. These last five years have seen the disappearance of unbraked and most vacuum-braked wagons from Scotland. The main line freights include steel from Ravenscraig and Gartcosh on air-braked flats; lime for the blast furnaces in BSC-owned hoppers and tipplers; cement in bogie hoppers; and cars, pet food, whisky and a host of commodities in the expanding Speedlink network. Many of these trains are double-headed by electric locomotives in multiple.

For safety's sake, now that there are virtually no lineside signalboxes on the Scottish part of the route, the use of strategically placed hot-axlebox detectors enables the very occasional train with a suspect vehicle to be looped clear so that attention can be given to it while other traffic continues by.

Almost unseen by the general travelling public are the overnight van trains that carry our mails, parcels and newspapers. Made up of specially-built sorting and storage vans are the Post Office trains, the southbound star of which leaves Glasgow Central each night at 19.30 for London. This is a full-length train on which on-train mail sorting is still practised. Another group of night van trains that are accorded high customer priority are the newspaper trains, which use the West Coast route for all Scottish destinations. These are formed from specially selected ex-GUV vans run at tight timings from London and Manchester to the four main Scottish cities as well as other towns en route. Close watch is maintained by both Regions responsible for their operation to ensure punctual running – late newspapers don't sell well!

Decisions will no doubt soon be made as to the maintenance strategy to be adopted for the InterCity 225 trains. At present, electric locomotives are maintained at Willesden depot (Classes 86 and 87) and Crewe (Class 85) in England; only the Class 81 is maintained in Scotland, at Shields depot, Glasgow. Mk 3a carriages on the Anglo-Scottish services are based at Willesden, and most of the Mk 2s at Polmadie, though short-term environmental attention is given at whichever depot a train ends up at over night.

Overall the West Coast main line picture is of a resumed pattern of steady, medium-term improvement, with the prospect of regaining by the end of the decade its former proud position of Britain's 'Premier Line'.

Top:
Nine 45-ton covered limestone hoppers (locally known as 'white ladies') head south across Harthope viaduct behind No 81.014 on 27 August 1979. The northbound workings of these wagons carry limestone from quarries at Shap to the Ravenscraig steelworks.
D. G. Cameron

Above:
Preparing for a run in which a maximum speed of 155.6mph was reached near Whamphrey, an Advanced Passenger Train formation pauses at Quintinshill in April 1980.

Right:
An Inverness-based Class 26 Bo-Bo brings a postal train from the north of Scotland to London into Motherwell in 1976.

Top:
After electrification made possible a fast evening train journey to London, the 17.30 to Euston was Glasgow's prime evening departure. No 87.034 *William Shakespeare* threads this train through the Central station throat in May 1978.

Above:
Since early 1985, the principal West Coast route 110mph trains have been full Mk 3a formations decked in the new InterCity colours, two-tone grey with white-and-red stripes.

Left:
Glasgow is a major centre for the Freightliner container business. In this 1976 view of Gushetfaulds depot, a powerful 10,000hp combination of two Class 87 electric locomotives pulls slowly away with a 20-wagon overnight train (max 1,600 tons) for London's Willesden terminal.

Top:
Having to surmount two high railway summits (Shap and Beattock) can bring Euston-Glasgow trains into contact with some awful winter weather! The 13.50 from London on 13 December 1981 arrived at Glasgow Central encased in frozen snow and ice.

Left:
Glasgow Central's frontage in Gordon Street has been much admired since the Central Hotel building was stone-cleaned and the cab road awning repainted in sympathetic Victorian style.

Above:
In the early 1980s several new destinations were added to the timetable of trains heading south from Glasgow and Edinburgh which joined up at Carstairs. In this view, No 86.224 *Caledonian* heads the inaugural 'European' out of Glasgow Central, the train being bound for Manchester, Nottingham and, for the first time, Harwich Parkeston Quay.

17

2
High Speed Success

Whoever would have thought 10 years ago that by the early 1980s Edinburgh would have an hourly-interval service to King's Cross using diesel traction at speeds substantially exceeding those possible on the electrified West Coast route? Yet such is the success of BR's InterCity 125 high speed train (HST) that traffic on the line from Edinburgh to Newcastle and beyond to London (the northern end of which Dr Beeching had wished to close) fully justifies such an intensive service, to the point of the embarrassment of overcrowding at peak travel times on some trains.

The ingredients of this business surge are threefold. Journey times between the capitals have been slashed by the IC125s to 4½ hours for the 393 miles. With the hourly interval this creates new travel opportunities as well as competing harder with air travel. Secondly, the trains look good and are a quality product throughout. Being unit trains this quality is consistent. Thirdly, the train staff, particularly in catering, provide a reliable, cheerful and complete service.

While the East Coast main line is generally less scenically spectacular than the West Coast route, the Scottish end has some outstandingly beautiful stretches. North of the border beyond Berwick-on-Tweed the route takes the railway close to the cliff edge, giving superb views of cliffs, rocks and the North Sea. Further north the countryside is hilly and wooded, and further on still the line drops through rolling farmland and skirts the southern shore of the Firth of Forth, offering glimpses of wide sandy beaches near Dunbar.

The approach to Edinburgh is fast, with the Portobello Freightliner terminal and the modern, well-equipped HST and carriage maintenance depot at Craigentinny flashing past before the train slows to pass the Meadowbank stadium (built on the site of the former St Margaret's steam locomotive depot). Then the pace slows to 20mph, the train enters Calton tunnel and emerges in the centre of the city, in Waverley station.

Waverley's central location is as much a problem as it is a boon. Its 21 platforms are crammed in a narrow cutting flanked by high stone walls (now stone-cleaned to considerable effect) and hemmed in by tunnels at each end. It is however but a short walk to Princes Street and its shops on the north side, and to the old city, the Royal Mile and the castle on the south (the station actually lies aligned east-to-west). The layout of the station's public areas has its difficulties, being dominated by a large central services and administration block, round which many passengers have to trail between connecting trains. Many improvements have however been made for the passengers, including a new travel centre, a warm, covered waiting area, tiled concourse, Solari train

departure and arrival indicators, a refurbished buffet and a computerised timetable information unit.

North of Edinburgh the majority of trains to Aberdeen are formed from Anglo-Scottish train sets: some are InterCity 125 workings, usually to and from London King's Cross, but one features a Leeds destination, and one locomotive-hauled set comes from Penzance! The balance is made up from Scottish internal stock. Service frequency is roughly every two hours from Edinburgh to Aberdeen, with Glasgow-Aberdeen trains dovetailed northwards from Dundee to provide a near-hourly interval around the Grampian coast.

Leaving Edinburgh the line passes, between tunnels, through the attractive Waverley Gardens, past the Haymarket locomotive depot next to the Murrayfield rugby football stadium, and veers away from the Glasgow line near the airport. This is the route of the great bridges. Crossing the Forth Bridge the railway is very high above the level of the Firth and affords superb views in both directions. The railway then drops through rocky outcrops into Inverkeithing and crosses Fife, first threading the coastal towns and then striking north to gain the Tay estuary at Wormit. The Tay Bridge is even longer than the Forth and, again, the traveller has good views along the Firth before the train swings round to join the line from Perth outside Dundee station.

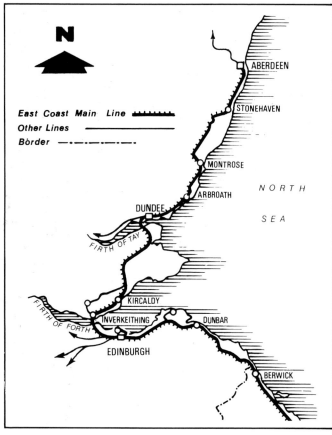

Beyond Dundee the land is essentially agricultural, undulating such that high speeds are not possible. Making use of the HSTs' lower track stresses, the Scottish Region has permitted them higher curving speeds than locomotive-hauled trains, with accordingly substantial journey time gains in 1982 and 1983. Arbroath, Montrose and Stonehaven are all coastal stopping places. Near journey's end the rocky North Sea cliffs give way to the modern tower blocks and traditional cold grey granite of Aberdeen. On the left can be seen the now small locomotive

servicing depot at Ferryhill, and as the train drops into the city and approaches the main station it passes the very small shed used to examine coaching stock.

Aberdeen station itself has a classic Scottish architectural style. At the Edinburgh end long bay platforms can accommodate full length InterCity trains. Alongside, the long through platform is able to link InterCity arrivals with the short trains that continue northwest to Inverness. The concourse is wide, tiled and, of course, in common with other Scottish East Coast route stations, it is now run as an 'open station' with no barrier queues.

Nearby is the Freightliner depot, a small one as such are, but which maintains connections via Glasgow's Gushetfaulds depot with the rest of the BR network. Route clearances have just been improved to enable the now standard 8ft 6in high containers to reach Aberdeen on standard Freightliner wagons. Until now special arrangements have had to be made to carry these on 'lowliner' wagons, which exist only in limited numbers. Aberdeen is also the starting point for the now famous mixed train that conveys a Freightliner wagon for the far north at the front of the 13.45 passenger train to Inverness.

Further south there is considerable freight activity in the Lothian area. At Oxwellmains near Dunbar there is a large cement distribution centre which receives cement in bulk from the south. Nearer Edinburgh is Leith whose docks area contains Scotland's busiest general freight depot. A wide range of commodities passes through it including grain, coal, chemicals and, most significantly, gas mains pipes which are coated in the vicinity and distributed throughout the UK by rail.

As has been said already, the introduction of differential speed restrictions for HSTs since 1982 has enabled journey times to be cut. At the time of writing the fastest London to Aberdeen run is 6 hours 59 minutes. As a result passenger business is booming, fed by the oil industry, and the capacity of the HST sets is a problem at peak times. More second class trailer cars have been delivered to bring the remaining seven-coach sets up to eight vehicles, and replacement of the second catering car in other sets by a full second class saloon will further improve seat availability.

The Scottish Region has made better use of InterCity 125 sets in recent years. Originally, those due to leave Edinburgh for the south in mid and late morning waited at Craigentinny until near departure time. Now, one starts back at Dundee to replace a suburban diesel multiple-unit working, and another, which in 1982 started back at Perth, now overnights at Inverness. A third set runs to Glasgow in the morning peak and forms a Glasgow Queen Street to King's Cross train, a very popular departure from Queen Street because of the through service it provides for northeast England and Yorkshire.

The future has exercised BR's best management brains. The long awaited electrification was authorised in 1984 and opens several opportunities. Debate centred on the alternative forms of traction: should it be an electric HST, or should electric locomotive haulage be used? The latter has great advantages during the years when the wires move progressively north, so that diesel locomotives can take over trains at the northern extremity of the advancing electrification. However, diesel haulage using any of the existing types (Classes 47 or 50 being the only really suitable ones) has a penalty in Scotland because the speed advantage which HSTs have on curves is summarily lost. The prospect that electrification will not improve journey times beyond Edinburgh is not acceptable in Scotland. However at the time of writing the reported choice appears to be electric locomotives working in push-pull mode, surely the best way to achieve the advantages of unit trains and achieve tightly-timed locomotive changes where necessary. A non-tilting version of the InterCity 225 is also a strong contender.

Decisions on the types and detail of rolling stock to be used will be reached, probably, while this book is being printed. The passenger may well be able to look forward to such improvements as automatic exterior doors, 'active' suspensions for an even smoother ride, access to train-borne video, and information technology.

What is clear is that with loadings and frequencies already high on the route, future gains from reductions in costs will be just as important as the ability to run longer trains at 125mph with electric haulage. For this is one major route that must continue to earn a substantial profit for the InterCity sector and for BR.

Above left:
A High Speed Train presents the modern face of the 'Flying Scotsman', which in 1978 was the 10.10 departure from Edinburgh Waverley.

Left:
Before the InterCity 125s came on the scene, the East Coast main line expresses were dominated by the popular 'Deltic' diesel-electrics. Here, No 9011 *The Royal Northumberland Fusiliers* leaves Edinburgh's

Waverley station with the up 'Talisman' on 3 June 1972.
J. H. Cooper-Smith

Above:
The railway threads through the heart of Edinburgh past Princes Street gardens. In these pleasant surroundings No 40.136 approaches Waverley with a Freightliner set from Dundee or Aberdeen, for Portobello terminal, on 4 May 1979.
G. A. Watt

Top:
The East Coast main line follows a precarious course above the cliffs at Burnmouth, north of Berwick, the location of more than one landslip. On 23 April 1984 the 11.00 from King's Cross to Edinburgh passes this attractive North Sea coast.
Mrs Mary Boocock

Above:
A High Speed Train passes Burnmouth on the 14.00 from Edinburgh to London King's Cross in April 1984.

Right:
Following a cliff fall at Burnmouth the tracks were sharply slewed around the collapse by the civil engineer's staff. This view shows the 08.00 from Edinburgh gingerly passing the scene on 13 June 1983, before a permanent 90mph diversion had been engineered further away from the cliff edge.

Left:
Britain's longest railway bridge is the Tay bridge, between Dundee and the Fife peninsular. As the 17.21 to Edinburgh heads on to the bridge behind No 47.210, the bases of the original bridge piers come clearly into view.
Tim Boocock

Below:
The great gantry of semaphore signals outside Aberdeen station has now given way to multiple-aspect signalling worked from one central signalling centre nearby. As the 11.40 push-pull train of 7 April 1981 departs for Glasgow, a Mk 2 coach is given attention in the small carriage shed, used at night to service HSTs.

Bottom:
A humble ballast train approaches Markinch behind one of the Class 40 1Co-Co1s still surviving in Scotland in May 1979.

3
ScotRail Main Lines

The ScotRail main line services north of Glasgow and Edinburgh form a cohesive group, particularly since the basic interval timetable was established across the Region in 1982. The half-hourly Edinburgh-Glasgow push-pull service is interwoven between two-hourly Glasgow-Aberdeens and the more irregular services from Edinburgh to Perth and Inverness. The Glasgow-Aberdeens also interweave north of Dundee with the East Coast route trains from Edinburgh to Aberdeen. The attempt to lock on to an hourly interval between Dundee and Aberdeen has not yet been entirely successful because of the less-than-regular pattern of East Coast route trains from over the border. Nonetheless, considering the distances involved, a very reasonable service is provided.

A conundrum is that all these trains have been carrying the InterCity motif on their coaches, most of which are air-conditioned, but the routes all form part of BR's Provincial sector. This is a major reason why BR's smallest Region contributes a disproportionately large share of the revenue and costs of that sector. Indeed the Edinburgh-Glasgow and the two Aberdeen routes manage to provide a useful contribution to overheads. On recently repainted coaches the InterCity name is replaced by 'ScotRail'.

For the sake of completeness, the Aberdeen-Inverness route is also included in this chapter.

The two great cities of Edinburgh and Glasgow are respectively Scotland's administrative capital and its commercial and industrial centre. Over half of Scotland's five million people live in the central belt or within reach of one or other of the two cities. Both are great centres for tourism, Edinburgh having its castle, the Royal Mile, Holyrood House and Princes Street; Glasgow has its fine, well-preserved Victorian city buildings and its scenic hinterland. The inter-dependence of their economies results in considerable two-way traffic between them, an ideal bedrock for a successful rail passenger service.

In the early 1970s the so-called inter-city diesel multiple-units which plied between Edinburgh and Glasgow were not holding traffic in competition with the motor car. At over an hour for the 47 miles with one or two intermediate stops, timings were not competitive door-to-door, so push-pull trains were formed using pairs of Class 27s, one at each end of six disc-braked Mk 2 coaches. Quite intensively worked, with timings around 45 minutes, this much-improved service was instantly successful but took its eventual toll on equipment reliability. Maintenance of the locomotives was expensive – particularly running and brake gear – the Deutz-engined diesel-alternator sets couldn't cope reliably with the train heat load in the coldest winters, and the high

Sir Walter Scott, No 47.710, brings the 10.30 from Glasgow round the base of Edinburgh castle's rock near journey's end on 26 April 1983.

braking rate (6%g and 12%g in stages) caused much wheel damage which in turn upset the availability of the coaching stock. In the late 1970s staff confidence dropped and the service performance reached seriously low levels. This naturally rebounded on other services penetrating elsewhere in the Region and action had to be taken.

New General Manager Leslie Soane obtained Board authority to acquire 34 up-to-date Mk 3a coaches from the LM Region, and to modify in BREL 12 Class 47/4s and 10 Mk 2f BSOs (there were no Mk 3a brake vehicles on BR) for push-pull operation. The push-pull control chosen used the train's lighting wires, fed through new jumper cables from the locomotive, to support an electronic time-division-multiplex system. Each locomotive (renumbered in the '47/7' series) was fitted with a receiver to translate coded pulses into normal control operations. The BSOs were rebuilt with half-width cabs and fitted with encoders and transmitters linked to their simple EMU-type controllers. Their second class passenger compartments were carpeted to match the Mk 3a stock with which they were to work.

Once all six 6-car train sets, and the odd spare vehicles, had been introduced there was a quantum leap in reliability. Timekeeping rose to the 95% right time mark, 100% on some days, just soon enough to hold on to traffic levels in the face of the economic recession and the M8 motorway extension into Glasgow. In 1981, confidence in potential utilisation had risen to the point that by re-diagramming the five train sets that worked each day it proved possible for one set, with the addition of a buffet car, to cover two out-and-back Glasgow-Aberdeen runs. In addition to this, a spare '47/7' and DBSO were marshalled around five early air-braked Mk 2 coaches to provide an additional peak service set. So flexible is the two-wire system that any standard air-braked passenger coach can be inserted in the formation. The push-pull trains have been repainted in the ScotRail version of the new InterCity livery.

A passenger from Edinburgh to Glasgow gifted with a cab pass joins the driver at Waverley. With the cab interior door of the DBSO swung back across to close off the cab from the brake van, a virtual full-width cab is created, with a good view forward also from the non-driving side. At the right-away, forward acceleration is brisk though silent as the unmanned locomotive roars to itself over 440ft away at the rear. A brief stop at the modernised Haymarket station is followed by full throttle acceleration past the locomotive depot, the Murrayfield rugby football ground and the airport, as the Glasgow line heads westwards. One of the oldest passenger railway routes in Scotland, the Edinburgh-Glasgow line of the North British Railway was in most respects well engineered and its alignment in difficult country was superb. For the most part it is now capable of supporting 100mph running, at which speed the '47/7s' were passed to run in 1984.

We pass the new industrial estates near Livingstone, and cross a very long masonry-arch viaduct. The link from the Forth Bridge and Dalmeny trails in from the right just after the awkward tunnel at Winchburgh. Past Polmont the Falkirk Grahamston loop (and the link to Stirling) leaves us on the right and soon we plunge into Falkirk tunnel, brake, and stop at Falkirk High station. This is one of a number of stations rebuilt when the Edinburgh-Glasgow service was upgraded and is an architecturally delightful modern station with small sandstone buildings.

Soon after Falkirk the main line from the north trails in from the right. To the north lie the central highlands, and as we continue west at 90-100mph the Campsie Hills run parallel to us for miles. Now in the Strathclyde PTE area we flash through Croy, Lenzie

and Bishopbriggs stations, the brakes go on and we curve through a deep rock cutting to emerge with Eastfield, Scotland's largest diesel depot, on our left. Then it's down at 1 in 40 through the tunnel to Glasgow's Queen Street station.

Queen Street is one of Britain's most attractive major termini. It has a wide, single-span, arched roof, the cladding between the glazing painted light blue. Its well-proportioned concourse is now terrazzo-tiled and the platform barriers have been removed. This, and an intelligent grouping of illuminated advertisements, has brightened its appearance considerably.

Queen Street is the starting point for the Glagow to Aberdeen and Inverness services. These share tracks with the Edinburgh route as far as Greenhill where they turn north, pass through the rebuilt station at Larbert, and enter the highlands at Stirling. From there the line climbs through Dunblane and emerges on a broad open expanse of marshy land that in winter is host to thousands of migratory geese from the Arctic regions. Superbly green and undulating country around Gleneagles gives way to a broad, arable valley flanked by high hills, through which the railway drops steadily before diving into Hilton tunnel at the approach to Perth.

Perth's enormous station is too large really for today's traffic. To move it to an easier site, or to demolish it and rebuild where it is, would be too costly. It is in any case centrally placed for the city, so BR has accepted the need to keep it well maintained and has modernised the entrance, booking and buffet areas.

Aberdeen trains call at the sharply curved platforms on the east side and then make their way across a single line bridge over the River Tay; then they follow the Tay bank with its salmon fisheries, to join the East Coast route at Dundee.

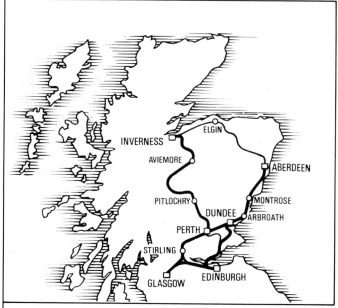

For Inverness travellers the Highland line proper starts at Perth. This is a very grand route scenically, not as beautiful as the lines to Kyle or Fort William, but with a formidable character of its own. Its trains are dwarfed by their surroundings as they climb to and breast Druimuachdar summit, 1,481ft above sea level. Trains call at most of the few stations en route but only Pitlochry and Aviemore are in any way populous. After dropping into Aviemore, trains are faced with another long climb to Slochd summit before descending steeply across Culloden Moor. The view across the Moray Firth is spectacular and includes the road bridge to the Black Isle which has formed part of the very expensive A9 trunk road link to the far north. This road is used at low cost by many modern luxury coaches.

Even Inverness station has received the full 'customer first' treatment with an exceptionally bright concourse, travel centre, micro-dot train indicator and modernised buffet. It was one of BR's first 'open stations' and is now completely without barriers. It forms the gateway to the far north – for even here the determined traveller can still be 161 miles short of his rail destination!

In the mid-1970s, Mk 1 stock gave way to vacuum-braked Mk 2 coaches on Scotland's internal InterCity trains, and the Glasgow-Aberdeen service was grouped into a basic two-hourly pattern, with a three-hour journey time. In the last 10 years this service has been transformed, Class 40s being replaced by 47s, vacuum braked Mk 2s being displaced by air-conditioned Mk 2d stock. Timings were cut to two hours 45 minutes by selective raising of track standards and speed limits, and by reducing formations from seven to six coaches and replacing RMBs by TSOTs. The latest move, to form them into push-pull sets, adds further to economy and reliability in operation. Thus Aberdeen, the oil capital of Britain, is served by modern air-conditioned trains from both Glasgow and Edinburgh.

Inverness, being a smaller centre and yet further away, cannot support such a regular service pattern. It has three basic InterCity service groups. The Anglo-Scottish day trains are the 'Clansman' to Birmingham and the 'Highland Chieftain' InterCity 125 introduced in 1984 direct to Edinburgh and King's Cross. At night the 'Royal Highlander' conveys Mk 3a sleeping cars to London Euston, and there is a mixed sleeping and seating train as well. The third service group (actually part of the Provincial Services sector) is that to Glasgow and Edinburgh, formed by Class 47/4 locomotives hauling Mk 2 pressure ventilated air-braked stock. This is balanced at night by single Mk 3a sleeping cars attached to the overnight trains to and from both cities. It is this third group that has been most sharply challenged by the coach operators in the early 1980s.

Aided by the well-engineered A9 trunk road, motor coaches can challenge the overall rail timings, and offer new vehicles of considerable amenity at very low fares. To hold on to its market share, ScotRail in 1983 launched a £5 single journey fare from Glasgow and Edinburgh to Inverness. This competition expanded the market and BR supported it with an additional train on summer Fridays, a peak travel day. This was formed by the Mk 2 push-pull set and named the 'Jacobite'. Lest readers leap to their rostra and proclaim the overall benefits of low fares for all, let me at once say that all this only served to hold on to BR's market to ride the recession – it is not a profitable operation by any yardstick, not even for the buses, some of which have since been withdrawn.

Road competition on the Edinburgh-Glasgow route cannot meet the railway's performance on timings, nor on reliability, though Stagecoach did launch an hourly run in 1983 with the slogan 'This is the age of the Stage!' (Imitation is the sincerest form of flattery.)

To encourage tourism further, summer passengers on the 'Clansman', very much an optional market train, hear a pleasantly spoken narrative outlining points of historic and scenic interest as they proceed between Inverness and Perth. This is a service provided jointly by BR and the Highlands & Islands Development Board and is supplemented on this and other day trains to Inverness by tartan-clad hostesses who distribute tourist literature and provide copious advice to a most appreciative clientele.

Freight on the northern lines is remarkably buoyant. Aberdeen is on the Freightliner network and in 1983-84 BR invested to achieve clearances for 8ft 6in containers to reach it. Inverness is not far south of Invergordon's industrial estates and has some of its own, fed by BR's air-braked wagon fleet from Speedlink, and by block company trains of minerals, and grain for the whisky industry. Almost every town station between Aberdeen and Inverness boasts a yard in which the traveller (on his '47'-hauled two-hourly Mk 2 service) can glimpse modern wagons of surprising variety.

It was the expected increase in freight from the oil-based industries at locations such as Invergordon which prompted the investment in reinstatement of passing loops and double trackage on the Highland main line in the late 1970s.

The latest innovation is the use of an air-braked container flat behind the locomotive of a vacuum-braked Aberdeen-Inverness passenger train. This wagon has through vacuum and steam pipes and both brakes on the train work together successfully. Therefore a container flow from Aberdeen to Wick can be assured, without bearing the cost of special freight locomotives and crews.

In the central belt near Falkirk is the oil refinery and port of Grangemouth from which trains of loaded tank cars flow in various directions for distribution of fuel and gas oils. Freight, together with DMUs on Glasgow-bound services, and the internal InterCity trains just described, make the two tracks between Cowlairs and Greenhill the most intensely occupied main line in Scotland. Not surprisingly therefore, the Edinburgh-Glasow line is fully track-circuited, and signalled for 100mph running over much of its length.

New signalling centres have been commissioned in recent years at Edinburgh and Aberdeen. Semaphore signals still exist in pockets, for instance between the Carmuirs triangle (between Falkirk and Stirling) and Perth; over the Highland main line; and on the Aberdeen-Inverness line. Even at these places there are useful examples of modernisation. The crossing loop at Carrbridge, for example, is controlled remotely from Aviemore and the loop signals remain unlit until a train movement is set up. The Region aims to eliminate semaphore signalling and absolute block control completely by 1990.

The future of these lines clearly depends on regular government support through the Public Service Order grant. To justify this, BR has to continue seeking ways of making the services more attractive in the face of aggressive competition from road buses, the A9 and the motor car. For the time being the cascading of more modern coaching stock to the Scottish Region has almost ceased. Improvements are being applied from within, therefore, and these include the widespread fitting of public address equipment. ScR's aim is to have this on all internal locomotive-hauled stock in the north very shortly. There is also the judicious use of yellow paint to brighten the formerly dark-wood-panelled entrance vestibules of Mk 1 and 2 coaches, and the fitting of fluorescent lighting to rid the area once and for all of the dim 'gold-fish bowl' lighting of the early Mk 1 stock. And all vehicles are having applied to them the proud legend – *ScotRail*.

Above:
Glasgow Queen Street station occupies a very compact site as can be seen in this view. No 47.712 prepares to leave with the 13.30 push-pull to Edinburgh on 30 April 1981.

Left:
The western approach to Waverley station epitomises Edinburgh's classic outlines. Above the Mound tunnel is Scotland's national gallery while the castle sits broodily in the background. One of the former double-locomotive Mk 2 push-pull sets is just arriving, in March 1978.

Below left:
The new ScotRail colours give a striking appearance to this push-pull set from Edinburgh emerging into the stone-cleaned approaches to Glasgow Queen Street in December 1984.

Left:
There is much activity at Queen Street this morning (8 September 1982) as an HST prepares to leave on the 09.05 to Edinburgh and London King's Cross. Nearby is a Class 47/4 on the 09.25 to Aberdeen, a Class 26 backing in an empty West Highland set, a '47/7' on the 09.00 to Edinburgh, and a local DMU.

Below:
At Leuchars in Fife, No 47.274 arrives with a train from Aberdeen to Edinburgh on 14 April 1979.

Above:
On the Inverness-Aberdeen line, Class 26 Bo-Bo No 26.044 is seen on a passenger train between Kennethmont and Insch, probably in 1980. *C. J. M. Lofthus*

Left:
The Highland main line's longest daytime train journey nowadays is the 'Clansman', from Inverness to Birmingham and London Euston. It is seen here passing Druimuachadar summit on BR's highest railway (1,481ft above sea level) on 21 July 1984 behind No 47.423.

Above right:
A heavy southbound Speedlink freight train unusually headed by Class 47 No. 47.708 *Waverley* passes the east coast port of Arbroath on 17 June 1985. *A. O. Wynn*

Right:
ScotRail's 'flagship' locomotive No 47.701 *Saint Andrew* stands at the head of an Edinburgh push-pull train at Glasgow Queen Street on 20 September 1985.

Above left:
Scotland's famous beverage, whisky, is brewed in the distillery at Dalwhinnie. On 7 September 1979 No 47.707 *Holyrood* passes there with the 09.05 from Glasgow to Inverness, which conveys Motorail traffic from Stirling. *G. A. Watt*

Far left:
The 08.20 from Inverness to Glasgow pulls away from Aviemore near Kincraig behind No 47.209 on 19 July 1984.

Left:
The 07.20 Inverness to London King's Cross is a new train formed by a High Speed Train set from May 1984. Called 'Highland Chieftain', it is seen here bombing away from Newtonmore on 19 July 1984.

Above:
To match bus competition, ScotRail rostered its Mk 2 push-pull set to the low-fare 13.03 'Jacobite' service from Edinburgh to Inverness. The train is seen here dropping down from Tomatin on 20 July 1984, Class 47/7 at the rear.

Right:
'The freight train now arrived at platform 1 is the 13.45 from Aberdeen!' So might be the announcement at Inverness, because ScotRail operates BR's first public train with mixed air and vacuum brakes. Behind No 47.118 is a loaded, through-vacuum-piped, air-braked container flat wagon, followed by five vacuum-braked Mk 2 passenger coaches.

4
Strathclyde's Transport

Unlike the counties of England and Wales, the upper tier of local government in Scotland consists of nine regional councils each with a wide geographical spread equivalent to several of the former counties. The largest of these is Strathclyde, which with a population of around 2½ million people embraces about half the Scottish population.

This human concentration is even more marked when one remembers that Strathclyde's territory includes the sparsely-populated mountains and islands of Argyll, Bute and Arran. This population mass centres on Glasgow and the surrounding towns of Paisley, Dumbarton, Coatbridge, Motherwell, Hamilton and Greenock, plus the people dispersed to the 'new towns' of East Kilbride, Cumbernauld, Irvine and Erskine. At the extremities are the dormitory towns of Ayr, Helensburgh, Lanark and Airdrie.

It is not surprising that a complex network of competing suburban railways was established here in the last century. It formed the basis of the rationalised but busy system that exists today.

In the mid-1970s the Greater Glasgow Passenger Transport Executive (GGPTE) was formed to channel local financial support for transport in the Glasgow and neighbouring districts and to co-ordinate policies. Formation of Strathclyde Regional Council as the passenger transport authority was followed by expansion of the PTE area to cover all the locations mentioned above, and the renaming of the PTE as Strathclyde Passenger Transport Executive (SPTE).

SPTE owns and operates the Glasgow city bus network (over 700 vehicles) and underground railway, and co-ordinates the business and operating specifications and financing of the Clyde ferries (Caledonian MacBrayne), outer-district buses (Scottish Bus Group) and suburban railways (BR) in its area. At the time of writing, this financial support is considerable (BR's share in 1984 was almost £30million), representing a significant burden on the rates in the region and on central government's rate support grant system. It certainly represents a very firm local commitment to the rail network.

Electrification of Glasgow's suburban system has been progressively extended since the Helensburgh-Airdrie route and branches, all north of the Clyde, were first energised in 1960. That route was based on the former LNER cross-Glasgow tunnel route under Queen Street station, and it was connected with the terminus by stairs from the low-level platforms. The parallel ex-LMSR route under Glasgow Central was closed in the Beeching era as an unsupportable duplicate facility.

The south side of the city was the next to benefit when electrification was opened from Glasgow Central terminus to

Above:
Strathclyde PTE supports DMU services out of Queen Street as far as Croy. On the left, a Class 101 set forms the 20.38 to Dunblane on 16 January 1985.

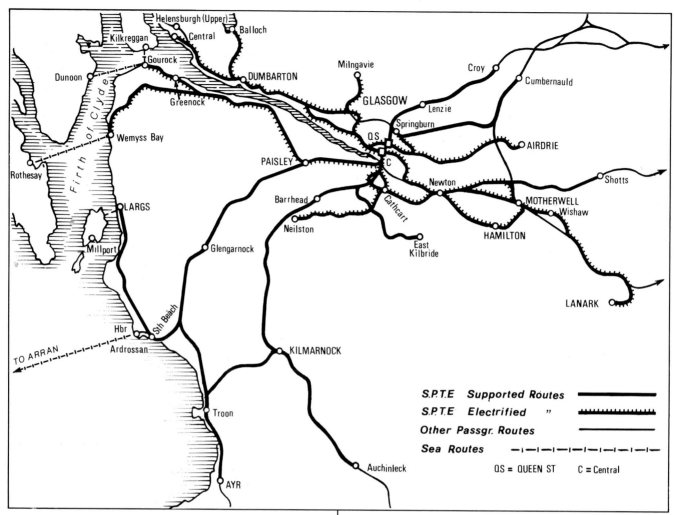

S.P.T.E   **Supported Routes** ▬▬▬▬

S.P.T.E   **Electrified**   " ⊣⊢⊣⊢⊣⊢⊣⊢⊣⊢

Other Passgr. Routes ▬▬▬▬

Sea Routes —ı—ı—ı—ı—ı—ı—ı—ı—

QS = QUEEN ST   C = Central

Motherwell via the Cathcart circle line and Kirkhill, and including the Neilston branch. By 1967 the wires had extended to Gourock and Wemyss Bay on the south shore of the Clyde estuary. The 1974 electrification of the northern end of the West Coast main line brought the Hamilton circle and the Lanark branch into the network.

The culmination of the PTE's early investment strategy brought two major injections of capital. The city's circular underground railway, which was still running with 80-year-old rolling stock, was to be completely re-equipped and modernised in all respects: track, stations, trains, workshops and signalling as well as operating methods. The result was a spectacular leap into the late 20th century on this popular 4ft 0in gauge route. Its regularity and reliability, together with the bright orange livery of its Metro-Cammell-supplied carriages, earned it the nickname 'Clockwork Orange' which has displaced the 'subway' tag by which it used to be known.

At the same time, BR was authorised to redevelop the former LMSR route via Glasgow Central low level station, to cross the Clyde between Dalmarnock and Rutherglen, and so provide a link between the north and south electrified systems across the centre of the city. This also has produced a modern railway with continuously welded slab track, brightly tiled stations and a batch of new electric multiple-units to provide the needed extra capacity. Services were revamped from November 1979 to produce a 10-minute interval through the tunnel, with trains running from Dumbarton and Dalmuir through to Hamilton and Motherwell, and Milngavie to Lanark. The new link was christened the Argyle line and was formally opened by Her Majesty the Queen in November 1979.

For the 1960s electrification, 110 three-car EMUs were built, many by the Pressed Steel Company of Linwood, Renfrewshire. Compared with contemporary EMUs in England, these had an up-to-date body design with sliding access doors, modern interior decor and, unusually for EMUs, a passenger view forward through the driving cab. They were launched with an original marketing package which included a 'Glasgow electrics' logo symbol of yellow and blue crossed arrows displayed on stations and prominent rail-over-road bridges. The trains themselves broke away from BR's sombre liveries by being decked out in Caledonian blue with black-and-yellow lining. Their impact was immediate and, apart from an early problem time when transformer troubles were being resolved, the 'blue trains' drew in good buisness.

An extra 16 sets were required for the Argyle line in 1979. These also broke new ground, being BR's first thyristor-controlled production EMUs. The Class 314s set new standards in ride, reliability and styling. They have actually also reduced maintenance costs compared with the Classes 303 and 311, as the batches of 'blue trains' subsequently became classified. They have, however, shown up the '303s' 1960s decor as dated.

The need was arising to consider the future of the '303s', in terms of whether to replace them in the 1980s or to rebuild them for an extended life. The latter course was chosen, and the PTE was able to obtain capital funding to support an initial programme of 50 sets, the first of which rolled out of Glasgow's BREL works in 1984. Interior decor is now up to Class 314 standard, and technical improvements have been made to increase reliability and to combat corrosion. By the time this book is printed, refurbished '303s' may well be working Scotland's first driver-only-operated BR passenger service. The Glasgow EMUs are maintained at depots at Shields and Hyndland.

Not all suburban lines around Glasgow are electrified. Notable exceptions are the Ayrshire routes to Ayr and Largs, the East Kilbride branch, services to Barrhead and Kilmarnock, Edinburgh via Shotts, Springburn-Cumbernauld and the routes out of Glasgow Queen Street high level to Croy, and beyond the PTE area to Stirling, Dunblane and Falkirk. All these are worked by standard three-car diesel multiple-unit sets, mostly of Class 101 (Metro-Cammell), but also some of Derby design and build of which Class 107 is unique to Scotland. Maintenance of these is based at Ayr and at Eastfield, Glasgow.

The Ayr route in particular has always been treated as an important commuter line. From the early days of dieselisation it was given Swindon inter-city DMUs (later known as Class 126) to provide a higher level of comfort. This was appreciated by many travellers, who were however less than happy when the '126s' were withdrawn in 1981-83. Body corrosion, the need for major rewiring and the presence of asbestos insulation were key factors in the sets' demise. Their replacements were Class 101 sets displaced from the Edinburgh-Dundee route, and redeployed '107s' released as a result of a re-diagramming exercise that reduced the amount of nine-car and six-car peak working in the SPTE area. All these sets had been refurbished with brighter decor and fluorescent lights and in these respects represented an improvement on the Class 126s.

The Ayr line is another line that carries lucrative two-way passenger traffic in the weekday peaks, between Glasgow, Paisley, Irvine, Troon, Prestwick and Ayr. Travel on the Kilwinning-Ardrossan-Largs branch tends to be more unidirectional: to Paisley and Glasgow on the weekday morning peaks, and towards Largs on warm summer weekends. The group is a relatively high revenue earner and supports a basic ½-hourly service to Ayr plus hourly trains to Largs, supplemented by extras in the peaks. It has for years been considered by BR Scottish Region to be a prime candidate for electrification and in 1983 authority was granted (supported by a 75% government grant for

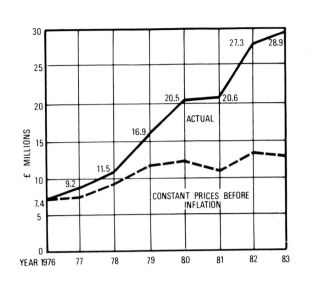

Above:
Graph depicting Strathclyde's spiralling S20 bill.

Below:
Graph showing how the Review proposes that S20 bills will come down.

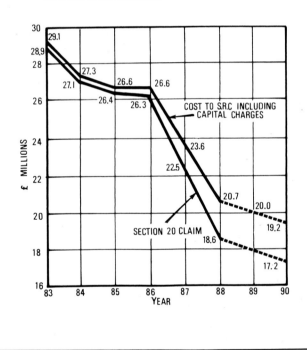

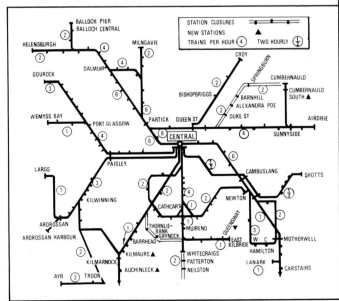

new rolling stock and a substantial sum from EEC funds) for the electrification works, covering the route to Ayr and the Largs branch as far as Ardrossan. Electrification to Largs was authorised in 1985. The scheme includes the construction by British Rail Engineering Ltd's York works of 20 Class 318 90mph outer-suburban EMU three-car sets.

The need to contain, and indeed reduce, the Section 20 grant payments by Strathclyde Regional Council led to the establishment of a joint working party to undertake a detailed review of future options for all the PTE's transport services.

Several radical alternatives were examined, including the effects of many line closures. The final report, published late in 1983, reflected the positive options put forward by BR Scottish Region's representatives on the working party. These included electrification to Cumbernauld from Coatbridge, thus dispensing with the Springburn-Cumbernauld DMU link and leading also to closure of the Springburn branch EMU service. East Kilbride would be reached by EMUs by relaying the chord line off the Neilston branch near Williamwood. The East Kilbride scheme received assent in 1985, but not the route to Cumbernauld.

DMU services would be increased to half-hourly to Barrhead and hourly to Kilmarnock, and this was implemented at the date of the May 1984 timetable change. Four new stations were to be opened across the network; two were achieved in 1984. Class 150 units would be bid for, to operate the residual non-electrified services to Barrhead and Kilmarnock.

Most fundamental to the reduction in call upon the public purse is the successive conversion of services to driver-only-operation. The first of these schemes incorporating a new Strathclyde manning agreement should be in operation very soon, using refurbished Class 303 units on the Gourock line. On completion of the plan, all other things being equal, the rail network subsidy under Section 20 will have been reduced by over 30% in real terms.

In the meantime, Scottish Region has not stood still in its efforts to meet competition from bus companies aiming to cream off some of the commuter business. The Gourock buses, competing against EMUs, have not apparently had a great effect on BR, but those in the Ayrshire corridor attracted much custom from BR's ageing DMUs. BR's response was original and simple: to provide air-conditioned InterCity stock on a principal peak working each way. By timing departure from Ayr at 07.55 it was possible to use the stock due to form the 09.10 'Royal Scot' from Glasgow to London Euston, and to market the train as a through Ayr-Euston service. This proved to be very successful. For the evening return to Ayr the stock for the 'Nightrider' service was put in for an out-and-back run, in good time to take up its later, overnight working. A valuable spin-off was the displacement of two three-car DMU sets for scrap.

Following the success of the Glasgow Underground with its orange train livery, SPTE experimented with an orange colour on the single-deck buses which linked Glasgow's Central and Queen Street stations, and later also on double-deckers that took over from the Paisley Canal line trains when they were withdrawn at the time of the closure of the Kilmacolm branch in 1983. This livery was refined to a brighter, deeper orange and is now being applied to all SPTE buses. (The colour, originally listed as 'Govan Orange' after the Underground's Govan headquarters, has been renamed 'Strathclyde Red', apparently a much more politically acceptable nametag in that area!) The colour is offset by a matt black band across the window area and looks very smart indeed.

This livery was adopted in 1983 for the EMUs in the SPTE area, with considerable visual impact, and late in 1984 it spread to the DMUs based at Ayr depot and which tend much less to wander away from the PTE area than do those at Eastfield. Also from 1984 the road overbridge signs near certain Glasgow suburban stations were progressively replaced by orange ones bearing the same 'Strathclyde Transport' logo as the trains and buses. The common livery emphasises the philosophy of an integrated bus/rail network, which is exemplified by the Interlink bus/train connections at stations such as East Kilbride and Johnstone.

By the time this book is published, the debate over deregulation of inner-city bus fleets may well have induced changes in Strathclyde's thinking on transport infrastructure. It is to be hoped that whatever is the outcome of the government's proposals, the comprehensive nature of the Strathclyde public transport system and its plans will continue to work for the benefit of the local population. They, after all, include a higher-than-average proportion of households with no access to private transport.

Below left:
As part of the 1979 modernisation scheme, Strathclyde Passenger Transport Executive funded the building of a new station at Partick to provide an interchange with its revitalised underground railway which the BR line crossed at this point.

Above:
The new station at Argyle Street presents a modern frontage to Glasgwegians walking along the main shopping street.

Above right:
Typical of stations on the south Glasgow circle line is the wooden 'pagoda' building at Cathcart. This building was totally modernised internally in 1982.

Right:
Who said you *had* to have colour light signalling in 25kV electrified areas? Semaphore signals survive on the Strathclyde system at Helensburgh, and at Milngavie as seen here. All will disappear when ScotRail's north Clyde resignalling scheme is authorised. *Brian Morrison*

Left:
Modern EMU No 314.215 pauses at Argyle Street station on a Motherwell to Dalmuir working in January 1984.

Below left:
A Class 116 DMU from Barrhead joins the two legs of the Cathcart circle line (left and right background) as they converge near Pollockshields East station.

Right:
The former 'Glasgow electrics' crossed arrow symbols (above right) survived into the 1980s . . . until replaced in 1984 by new Strathclyde Transport displays (right) on Strathclyde red backgrounds as seen here on a bridge by Langside station on 1 July 1984.

Below:
Life extension and refurbishing of the Class 303 EMUs has given a new image to the south Clyde services. Refurbished unit No 303.014 forms a Gourock line service on 17 January 1985.

Left:
Following unsatisfactory financial results, Strathclyde Regional Council withdrew support for the Kilmacolm branch line, which closed early in 1981.
Brian Morrison

Below left:
The Regional Council supported the opening of two new stations in 1984, this one being at Kilmaurs, north of Kilmarnock.

Above right:
Providing much better comfort for commuters, and in addition forming a through Ayr-London service, the 07.55 'Royal Scot' from Ayr to Glasgow and Euston passes Paisley behind No 47.562 *Sir William Burrell.*

Right:
The short gap between Glasgow's Central and Queen Street stations is filled by this PTE Rail-Link bus service.

Below:
A foretaste of things to come after electrification is completed to Ayr (due 1986) was provided for visitors to the Ayr railfayre on 29 and 30 October 1983, in the form of new EMU No 317.335.

5
The Eastern Network

In contrast to Glasgow where the suburban network is backed by a PTE through Section 20 payments, the Scottish capital of Edinburgh relies on the normal Public Service Order grant for the support of much of its rail commuter network. With the possible exception of Bristol, it is unique in this respect among the major UK cities. As a result, the system which was bequeathed to the area at the end of the 1960s remains virtually unchanged, and the improvements that have indeed been made have been largely a result of BR's initiatives. Certainly, close liaison is maintained with Lothian, Fife and Tayside Regional councils which take a lively interest in service quality and whose support is being encouraged for localised projects.

The archetypal Edinburgh suburban train is the three-car Metro-Cammell DMU, a formation that has been the backbone of services since the mid-1950s. Commuters arrive in Edinburgh from Dundee and the Fife coast towns and from Dunfermline and Inverkeithing in the north; from Dunbar and North Berwick on the East Coast main line; from Stirling, Falkirk and Linlithgow in the west; and from stations on the former Caledonian route from Glasgow via Shotts and West Calder. All services concentrate on Waverley station and most form convenient connections into and out of East Coast main line expresses.

Throughout most of this period the services into Fife have been organised on a fixed-interval basis with standardised hourly departure times and stopping patterns, at least on the services that cross the Forth Bridge. As a result they load well, but do peak quite seriously, morning and evening. The required strengthening of trains at peak times results in some under-utilisation of rolling stock. Concern that a recent decline in patronage was evidence of public resistance to DMUs for longer journeys led to plans to replace them by locomotive-hauled trains in 1981. Consequently the service pattern was adjusted so that each hour there was a locomotive-hauled semi-fast calling at Haymarket, Inverkeithing, Kirkcaldy, Markinch, Ladybank, Cupar, Leuchars and Dundee. In between were slotted DMUs stopping at all stations from Edinburgh to Kirkcaldy. Class 26s hauled four Mk 1 second class coaches on the semi-fasts, and these were upgraded to Mk 2 vacuum-braked stock in 1983. The Class 26s were replaced by '27s' for improved reliability from 1982. This action did appear to arrest the decline in patronage. In addition, Scottish Region's insistence on the completion of the refurbishing programme for its DMU fleet provided some improvement to the stock on the other routes, and the visual image was improved in 1981/82 by replacing the drab all-over rail blue livery by the brighter blue-and-grey, a lead followed soon after by the other Regions.

The 11.17 from Edinburgh to Dundee leaves Waverley behind Bo-Bo No 27.042 on 26 April 1983. Mk 2 vacuum-braked stock had been drafted onto this semi-fast service the previous month.

Services via Shotts to Glasgow Central are roughly two-hourly except during the peaks. At the western end they are supported by Strathclyde PTE, while Lothian Regional Council take an interest in the eastern end. A new station at Livingstone was opened in 1984.

To Dunbar and North Berwick there is a service which, again with support from Lothian, was started back from Haymarket in 1983 to form a cross-Edinburgh service.

The last (but not least) suburban service from Edinburgh is that to Falkirk and beyond. This has undergone several stages of experiment and development in recent years in an attempt to improve links with Linlithgow and Polmont in particular. Services normally run half-hourly as far as Stirling, with alternate, hourly trains extended to Dunblane. Each hour there is also a connection for Glasgow at Falkirk Grahamston (actually closer to Falkirk centre than is the High station on the main line). A few trains are extended to Perth and call at Gleneagles, though for this length of journey a Class 101 DMU is not ideal transport and so ScR has put its Mk 2 push-pull set in this roster, except on summer Fridays when it forms the 'Jacobite' train to Inverness.

Dundee is the centre of two other DMU links, the first a very sparse service along the Tay to and from Perth, and the second an hourly one calling at the many small stations along the coast to Arbroath. The latter is marketed under the brand name of Tayway with financial support from Tayside Regional Council. It used single diesel power cars for a few years until Scottish Region recognised that to keep four single power cars for two single-car diagrams was actually more expensive than running one three-car

set and rotating diagrams through Haymarket depot. In any case, rising patronage necessitated strengthening the single cars on many occasions.

The Dundee-Perth stopping trains had two intermediate calls, at Invergowrie and Errol, both of very limited business potential. Errol was closed in 1985.

An attempt was made in the early 1980s to invigorate suburban travel in the Aberdeen area. The active local branch of the drivers' union, ASLEF, put forward a proposal that morning and evening peak services from and to Stonehaven to the south and Inverurie and Huntly to the northwest would attract new custom to BR. A trial timetable was operated for a year, using a single-car DMU and a locomotive-hauled set on lay-over, to test the market. Regrettably custom did not cover direct costs and the experiment had to be curtailed, though in the 1984/85 timetable an InterCity train (to Penzance!) which starts back at Elgin does provide useful morning peak capacity.

The dependence on DMUs for suburban services around Edinburgh in particular will clearly go on for many years after the East Coast main line electrification. ScR therefore is bidding hard for its first non-PTE DMU replacements to come to Haymarket for these services. These are likely to be Class 150-type units with outer-suburban seating, and the better potential of these for higher utilisation and lower maintenance time will enable fewer new vehicles to work the same services, at substantially lower costs for a much higher standard of passenger comfort. Class 150s are being proposed also for the re-opening of train services to Bathgate in early 1986.

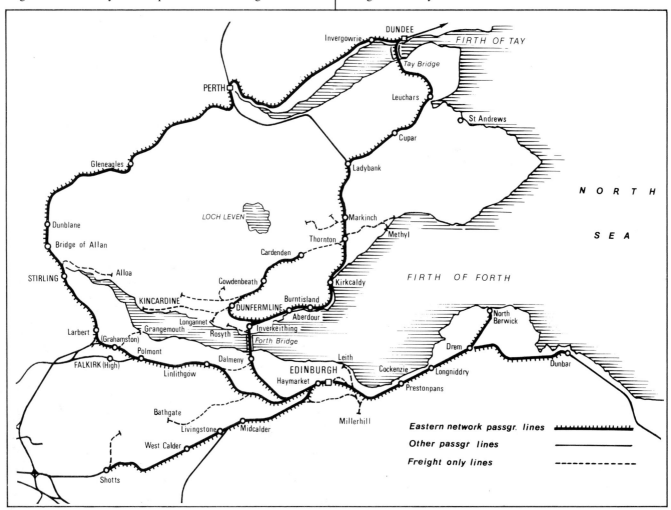

There is considerable freight traffic on the east side of the Region, some of which was referred to in the chapter on the East Coast main line. In addition to the aforementioned Freightliner, cement and Leith docks traffic, Lothian and Fife generate important flows of coal from indigenous mines, particularly to the modern power stations at Longannet and Cockenzie on the north and south shores of the Forth estuary.

Much of this coal traffic is fairly short-haul. The Monktonhall-Cockenzie flow is unique in that it uses single Class 26 locomotives that have been fitted for slow speed control for ½mph wagon loading and unloading operations, hauling HAA wagons fitted with canopies. Standard ScR power for MGR (merry-go-round) coal trains otherwise is two Class 20s in multiple, coupled with driving cabs outermost. These have also been modified, many years ago, with slow speed control of an ScR design, and much more recently with emergency brake valves in the cab. This latter feature allows the guard to ride on the second locomotive and thus dispenses with the brake van which these trains used to carry. A new proposal for radio control of the second locomotive will permit one Class 20 to be at each end of a MGR train, eliminating the need for running round at certain locations.

Longannet MGR trains at one time made up to over 40 wagons for extra capacity, and to cope with this load an extra Class 20 was coupled to the rear. Because it had its own engine crew, the third Class 20 actually increased the direct cost per ton payload. This practice was discontinued in 1983.

Observant travellers en route from Edinburgh to Dundee will have noticed a single line branch curving off the main line just south of Markinch station. This serves a number of mixed industrial locations. Because of the sharp curve by which it approached Markinch, this line was very restricted and until 1981 was worked by Andrew Barclay Class 06 0-4-0 204hp diesel mechanical locomotives. An easing of the curve that year enabled standard Class 08 0-6-0s to go down the branch and the '06s', the last in BR revenue earning service, were finally withdrawn (one going to Reading as a departmental locomotive).

Other Fife branch lines serve the Royal Naval dockyard at Rosyth and docks and industrial complexes at Methyl and Kirkcaldy.

The present freight volume is carried on block trains or on Speedlink services which make heavy use of modern, air-braked wagons. In former days the freight scene involved much marshalling of thousands of smaller, older wagons daily. In the 1955 modernisation plan new or modernised marshalling yards were laid out at Millerhill near Edinburgh, and Thornton in Fife between Cowdenbeath and Markinch. Scottish Region's largest wagon shops were at Townhill, Dunfermline, where in the mid-1970s 300 wagons passed through the shops each week. The change in working to modern wagons, and the replacement of the old wagonload freight workings by the Speedlink network reduced Townhill's workload until its closure became inevitable. From its closing in January 1983 a small mobile gang was sufficient to meet all wagon repairs arising in Fife, and even this was subsequently disbanded in favour of occasional visits by staff from Millerhill.

The two great marshalling yards at Thornton and Millerhill are now shadows of their former selves. The small shed set up at Millerhill for planned preventive maintenance of MGR wagons, on the other hand, has remained and its role expanded in recent years as it also covers maintenance of other air-braked wagon fleets. It is a minimal, covered facility, adequate for the low workload involved in keeping modern wagons on the road.

Below:
In the earlier era on this route a Class 101 DMU halts at Inverkeithing on a Dundee-Edinburgh working on 9 May 1979.

Above:
Unit No 101.364 comes off the Forth bridge to stop at Dalmeny on 2 April 1983.

Left:
In this picture taken on 30 June 1983, the array of semaphore signals at the west end of Dundee station has control of No 47.210 about to shunt stock for the 17.12 to Edinburgh, while No 08.761 is held on the adjacent track.
Tim Boocock

Below left:
A train of empty cement wagons for Oxwellmains (East Lothian) leaves Grangemouth on 19 May 1983, hauled by No 37.112.
Mike Macdonald

Top right:
At Longannet power station Class 20s Nos D8326 and D8327 ease a coal train over the unloading hoppers in August 1973.
Derek Cross

Centre right:
On the freight-only branch which joins the main line near Thornton, No 20.204 clatters through the site of the former Cameron Bridge station on 17 September 1982 with the daily return empties from Methil power station.
George C. O'Hara

Right:
One of the last surviving Barclay 204hp diesel mechanical 0-4-0s, No 06.008, hurries along the branch towards the main line junction at Markinch on 9 May 1979.

6
South-Western Lines

Glasgow Central was not traditionally the starting point for passenger trains to the southwest of Scotland. Trains of the Glasgow & South Western Railway used the Saint Enoch terminus nearby, but the rationalisation of Britain's railways in the 1960s closed Glasgow's Buchanan Street and St Enoch stations and concentrated all services on Central and Queen Street.

It was not difficult to divert G&SW line trains into Glasgow Central because link already existed between Strathbungo and Muirhouse Junction on to the tracks of the Cathcart circle line. The station certainly had capacity, a full 13 platforms with up to eight approach tracks across the bridge over the Clyde river.

Glasgow Central features a large concourse opposite the buffer ends of platforms 1 to 8, under acres of hipped, glazed roofing. Its polished timber-clad amenity buildings are listed as being of architectural interest, to which Scottish Region has responded by upgrading their condition and applying interior modernisation sympathetically. A major feature of the station was the train departure indicator, which used manually placed, pre-lettered boards and was clear to read and understand. Because it was so labour intensive, however, it has been replaced by a huge micro-dot board located across the buffer ends of the main line platforms, and the use of modern technology has enabled local repeaters to be sited at strategic locations all round the station. The place of the former board, at the upper level in the old 'torpedo building', is being taken by a new, high-quality Pullman lounge for first class passengers.

Other modernisation has already been undertaken. An excellent travel centre graces the station frontage, and booking offices, bar and buffets have all been brought up to date. The frontage itself, a tall grey sandstone structure of Victorian elegance, has been stone-cleaned and the entrance awning repainted with its delicate ironwork picked out in black, red and gold. Furthermore, although the concourse was not originally to be floor tiled because its sloping gradient was thought to render that dangerous in wet weather, a suitable tile surface has been found and laid. Later changes are planned which would segregate road vehicles and mails from passenger areas.

A few years ago the passenger for Stranraer and the boat connection to Northern Ireland would join a Swindon-built inter-city DMU (Class 126) at Glasgow Central forming part of the interval service on the Ayr line. After Ayr the character of the line changes from that of an outer suburban railway to become a single-track country by-way. The train climbs through farmland to Maybole and then drops, with the DMU clattering at speed along winding, jointed track, down into the harbour town of Girvan.

A panorama of Dumfries forms the background to No 47.535 *University of Leicester* on 20 July 1984 as it restarts the Stranraer-Euston day boat train away from a check at the south signalbox. *George C. O'Hara*

Here the line's character changes yet again. Out of Girvan the start is immediately on an up grade of 1 in 52 and our DMU roars away in second gear for over five miles as the railway climbs up from the sea and out towards the moors with spectacular views across towards Kintyre, Arran and the isolated islet of Ailsa Craig. From Pinmore tunnel the railway swings about to cross a wooded valley near Pinwherry and then climbs to emerge in wild moorland country. A brief halt at Barrhill is followed by the passage through more wilderness on well-laid continuously-welded rail. The few shallow cuttings through which we pass have proved vulnerable in winter to being filled with drifted snow. We drop down past New Luce, join the alignment of the former Carlisle-Dumfries-Stranraer direct line, and pass through the loop at Dunragit.

The approach to Stranraer reminds us of changes that have taken place. A low, modern, wide span building on our left is the transit depot of Stockton Haulage, a firm which uses rail for much intra-national traffic, particularly constructional steel. The alignment of the former route to Portpatrick (the original Irish-bound port in these parts) curves off to the left at the site of Stranraer Town station. We run on to the breakwater and stop in the harbour station with the *Ailsa Princess* or *Antrim Princess* on our right. The extended travels to which passage on one of these

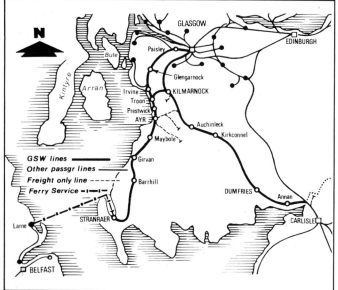

ships can lead us can (and perhaps will?) fill another book!

Dissatisfaction with DMUs for such a long journey, approaching three hours, led in 1982 to a decision to replace the '126s' by trains of Mk 1 stock hauled by Class 27 locomotives for the Glasgow-Stranraer services. The services were further developed in 1984 in two ways. The coaching stock was facelifted with fluorescent lighting and brighter decor, and Sealink paid BR to paint them in a striking red, white and blue livery that was also used on Northern Ireland Railways' boat train DEMU set, to provide the image of a co-ordinated link. Train timings were speeded up to about 2½ hours by using Class 47 locomotives, and running the Stranraer trains separately from the Glasgow-Ayr interval pattern enabled several stops to be cut out.

In addition to the Glasgow trains there are through Euston trains which go by way of Ayr and Kilmarnock, one sleeping car train at night and a Mk 2 air-conditioned train by day, plus a connecting service to Carlisle. In 1984 the harbour station was modernised to match the image being projected by Sealink's new facilities and

its new double-deck roll-on roll-off ferry *Galloway Princess*.

In many ways the other main ex-G&SW line is more of a problem. The Glasgow-Kilmarnock-Dumfries-Carlisle line trains serve intermediately few centres of population and therefore support a relatively sparse passenger service outside the Strathclyde PTE area; it also serves as a diversion route for West Coast main line trains, although not a very satisfactory one because journey times are extended by over an hour by its use. To encourage the route's retention, Scottish Region's approach is to maximise its revenue by providing road bus links to other towns, to reduce costs by further track singling, and to improve journey times by raising the line speed limit from 75 to 90mph. The bus links run from Dumfries to the Galloway towns, in similar fashion to the links from Carlisle to towns on the former Waverley route to Edinburgh.

The London-bound passenger from Northern Ireland has a roundabout route to follow, since the link from Stranraer to Dumfries was cut in the 1960s. His train from Stranraer travels north to Ayr, and then still further in the same direction until just after Troon. It then takes the right junction route at Barassie and runs at freight speed along the short single line, to reach Kilmarnock facing southwards. Climbing begins again at Kilmarnock to take the train through the high hills and through the scenic attractions of Drumlanrig gorge. In the author's view the visual impact of this route is finer than the West Coast main line north of Carlisle – less grand perhaps but abounding in wooded valleys, rolling hills and small farms.

The bulk of the main line was until recently still double track, being single only between Barrhead and Kilmarnock coming south from Glasgow, and between Annan and Gretna Junction where it joins the West Coast route and enters England. Other single line sections were added in the 1984 rationalisation. A number of single line branches can be seen joining the G&SW line at various points: these are freight only routes, most connecting the line with the collieries that form part of the Ayrshire coalfield. There is also freight from a branch in the Dumfries area that feeds into the Speedlink network.

After Dumfries the G&SW main line runs across flatter country as it approaches the northern shore of the Solway Firth, and calls at Annan before running under the wires into Carlisle. Here the diesel locomotive gives way to electric for the haul south to London.

The Ayrshire coalfield contains a small number of modern collieries which are linked to power stations on the east side of the country by trains of merry-go-round wagons headed by pairs of Class 20 locomotives. The decline of older mines has been matched by the development of opencast mining, a typical example being the mining complex near Dalmellington, southeast of Ayr. Formerly, a system of steam-worked railways linked the coal mines with a washery at Waterside, the coal from there being taken by BR in MDV end-door wagons down the steep branch line that joins the Girvan-Ayr line at Dalrymple Junction. Now that the mines are closed there is instead considerable open-cast working. This time big lorries are used to deliver the coal to Waterside, and BR's part is modernised, too: air-braked HBA wagons take the load to Ayr harbour where there is a hopper discharge point for the coal to be transshipped to sea transport.

Another port of considerable recent significance is Hunterston, between Ardrossan and Largs on the Clyde estuary, which has been developed by the British Steel Corporation to take bulk ore and coal-carrying ships of up to 250,000 tons. A large ore stacking area near the jetty feeds a conveyor belt system to reach the railway sidings which are up a hill, above the Largs railway. The loading hoppers can drop measured loads of iron ore into three 100-ton GLW wagons simultaneously so that a train of 21 wagons can be loaded in around half an hour. Two Class 37 diesels in multiple then take the 2,100-ton train the 50 or so miles via Glasgow to Ravenscraig steelworks near Motherwell. Imported Australian coal has been loaded and transported similarly, using HAA wagons loaded under a hopper alongside the ore hopper at Hunterston.

Other freight traffics on G&SW lines feed the ICI chemical complex at Stevenston near Ardrossan and another, new one near Dalry; finished steels via the Stockton Haulage depot at Stranraer; and general Speedlink trade. The author also recalls seeing a large timber finishing works and trains of tank wagons at Irvine.

Above:
The isolated islet of Ailsa Craig is prominent in this view of two Class 126 DMUs struggling up the climb from Girvan to Pinmore on 10 April 1982.

Left:
No 26.036 deputises for a Class 27 on the 08.35 from Glasgow to Stranraer on 9 October 1982, shortly after DMUs had been retired from the Stanraer trains.

Above:
The use of Class 47s enabled the Stranraer-Glasgow trains to be speeded up. With its coaches decorated in Sealink colours, a '47/4' passes Elderslie with the 13.35 northbound service. In the left foreground is the last surviving ex-G&SW signal, seen on 6 May 1984.
Mrs Mary Boocock

Left:
In former days at Stranraer, MV *Ailsa Princess* lies at berth after arrival from Larne on 16 September 1981. No 47.455 prepares to leave with the 13.15 to Carlisle. *Les Bertram*

Below left:
The station at Stranraer Harbour was modernised in 1984. No 47.597 is at the head of the 11.00 through train to London Euston.

Above:
Nos 20.089 and 20.139 amble uphill past the coal-mining village of Drongan with six empty coal hoppers from the La Roche factory at Dalry to Killoch colliery on 29 November 1983.
George C. O'Hara

Left:
Class 25 No 25.237 climbs past the village of Mossblown on 20 March 1980 with a rake of empty HBA coal hoppers from Ayr Harbour to Barony colliery.
George C. O'Hara

Right:
No 37.237 powers past Calowell on the G&SW main line with the thrice-weekly freight from Mossend Yard to Lugton and Giffen on 20 January 1984.
George C. O'Hara

Below:
Awaiting clearance at Mauchline Junction is No 37.147 with a trainload of caustic soda tanks from Stevenston on 12 June 1984.
George C. O'Hara

Above:
Iron ore from Hunterston for Ravenscraig passes Saltcoats seaside resort on 17 September 1981 behind Nos 37.125 and 37.148. The locomotives have 21 100-ton BSC tippler wagons in tow. *Les Bertram*

Right:
Another service from Hunterston to Ravenscraig is that which brings Australian coal to the steelworks. On 14 September 1981 one of these MGR trains had Nos 37.125 and 37.129 at its head as it passed the motor car terminal at Elderslie, near the former Linwood car factory. *Les Bertram*

Below right:
When engineering work blocks the West Coast main line, trains are diverted via the G&SW route via Kilmarnock. No 47.087 pilots dead electric locomotive No 86.223 on a Sunday Glasgow-Euston train, near Polquhap on 4 June 1978. *Derek Cross*

7
Roads to the Isles

To many people the mere mention of a Scottish railway conjures up foremost a picture of a single line winding among snow-dusted peaks past herds of deer and through acres of heather – a small Sulzer-engined Bo-Bo hammers along with three or four old carriages. An enthusiast's heaven? A tourist's ideal? What is the real picture?

Whenever people produce reports on the future of railways their proposals for rationalisation lead to many lines being omitted from maps. Always, the first cartographical sacrifices are the peripheral routes in the Celtic lands, be they for destinations at Llanelli, Aberystwyth, Pwllheli, or Oban, Mallaig, Kyle of Lochalsh, Thurso or Wick. Equally always, there ensues a loud political storm, and the railways' benefits to the nation are seen in a much wider light than mere financial viability. These railways that pass through few towns or settlements become of strategic importance: they are life-lines when roads are blocked with snow; they bring in tourists who otherwise might spend their money elsewhere and who boost the local economy; they connect sparse local industry to the outside world; and very often they serve marginal Parliamentary constituencies. On this tenuous thread their existence continues.

The best known of the Scottish routes in this category is the West Highland group of railways. The classic way for the English tourist to arrive in the Scottish highlands has been to take the overnight sleeping car from Euston. In days past our tourist would awaken while his sleeper was shunted at Glasgow Queen Street on to the 06.00 to Fort William. He might be shaving as the train rattled along the north shore of the Clyde, past Drumchapel, Dalmuir and Dumbarton, and would probably have walked through to the breakfast car by Garelochhead.

What better way can there be of starting the first day of one's holiday than by eating a hot, grilled breakfast in a railway restaurant car skirting the great lochs, Long and Lomond? The mist still hangs over the waters as the first rays of the sun strike orange on the mountain tops around, heralding one of those rarely glorious days that have put this fabulous countryside on thousands, nay millions, of calendars. Or perhaps, as the rain slashes across the moors on the climb to Crianlarich and the water streams down the carriage windows while the train's steam heating adds to the smell of dampness, our traveller wonders why he came? Many a holidaymaker has been deterred by the Scottish highlands' unpredictable weather, but most will agree, in retrospect, that this is truly a 'line for all seasons' (to quote BR's imaginative advertising), even though a trolley now has to suffice for the catering.

Above:
No 37.085 pauses at Arrochar and Tarbet while working the 08.04 Glasgow to Oban on 30 April 1983, waiting to cross a southbound train. This view illustrates the typical West Highland line station architecture.

58

After Crianlarich the train crosses a valley on a slender bridge on high piers and turns sharply to hug the north side of the glen, gradually climbing westwards above the level of the Oban line opposite. A brief halt at Tyndrum Upper (the smallest place in the British Isles with two railway stations) is followed by a turn to the north as the line climbs to a summit before dropping down round the famous horseshoe curve, a truly remarkable layout that uses the sides of a small glen to lose height in a curve that takes the railway through over 250 degrees. Then turning towards north again we call at Bridge of Orchy before setting out on the climb to Rannoch moor, the loneliest part of this route. Here it is possible to travel for miles without seeing a human soul: no road is within rescue distance should a train be stranded, whether by snowdrift or by the more mundane troubles which occasionally afflict old mechanical and electrical traction equipment. The moor is less barren now because drainage channels for afforestation have spread across its surface, leaving to the far north railway the distinction of passing through the wildest country.

Relative civilisation is reached as the line drops, now heading westwards to Roy Bridge and Spean Bridge. The train winds steadily through Monassie gorge and, continuing towards Fort William, the observant passenger may note what looks like a railway alignment on the hillside to the left of the train. Many have dismissed it as a well-engineered mountain track but it did carry, until the mid-1970s, a narrow gauge railway that serviced the reservoirs, sluices, tunnels, pumping stations and pipework of the Ben Cruachan pumped storage hydro-electric scheme.

Fort William emerges as an industrial centre, for in addition to the hydro-electric plant there is a large British Aluminium works whose raw materials and products use the West Highland railway for transport, and there is much other industry there.

Passengers arrive at Fort William at a new station completed in the 1970s on a new alignment about half-a-mile back from the earlier, restrictive terminus station at the lochside pier. This was a joint development which enabled the town's main street to be by-passed by a road along the former railway alignment. The new station is still within easy walking distance of the town centre and shops and affords a far better passenger environment.

The big attraction at Fort William is Ben Nevis, Britain's highest mountain at over 4,400ft. To see it from the train one needs to go beyond the town on the Mallaig extension railway. Tourists have been encouraged to use this line by the reintroduction of saloon cars in which a running commentary is given. A small supplementary charge is made. The first two saloons used were ex-LNER inspection vehicles, each of which had been given attention at Cowlairs carriage depot in Glasgow before transfer to Fort William, the first being named *Lochaber* at a ceremony there in 1981. Later this saloon was painted LNER beech brown by BREL at Toyota's expense so that it could take part in a steam train promotional run to Kyle. Cowlairs itself painted the second saloon, named *Loch Eil* in 1983.

Leaving Fort William the line turns west, leaving the Glasgow line near the small depot and traffic office complex, and crosses the Caledonian Canal at Banavie swing bridge. The ladder of canal locks that bring the boats down to sea level can be glimpsed here. Soon on the left the train passes the large pulp and paper mill at Corpach, part of which regrettably closed a few years ago. BR's traffic of cut timber from Crianlarich was terminated, but some output is still maintained and is loaded on to the regular Speedlink service. If the passenger looks back while the train skirts Loch Eil he may see the vast bulk of Ben Nevis looming over Fort William.

The next highlight is Glenfinnan, famous for the world's first concrete railway viaduct and for the view from it, because looking south the railway passenger has a perfect, classic view of Loch Finnan with Bonnie Prince Charlie's memorial at its head. Then the train winds through boulder-strewn hills and past more lochs and mountains towards the coast, passes the silver sands of Arisaig and Morar, and arrives unceremoniously at Mallaig, to find that, even at this small fishing village, ScotRail has felt it appropriate to provide updated station facilities.

In former years the Oban trains started from Glasgow's Buchanan Street station and headed through Cumbernauld and Stirling to join the Callander line at Dunblane. Now the Dunblane-Callander-Crianlarich Lower section is closed, following a landslide which effectively severed it, and trains use the even more attractive West Highland route as far as Crianlarich Upper.

The author took the Oban train in early January a few years ago. At Crianlarich the train had stopped for the locomotive to take water. Time was allowed here for diesels to replenish their steam heating boiler water tanks, a break often used by the train crew to visit the well-known, privately operated tea rooms in the station's island platform buildings. Our Class 27 pulled away into the snowy wastes, the train a dark streak against a white mountainscape. For some miles the Fort William line was visible higher up the opposite side of the valley, but after Tyndrum it turned north, away from us, as we continued to climb towards Glen Orchy. In the pass of Brander we noticed the semaphore signals that are held in the 'clear' position by the weighted wires of fences above the railways – a rock fall would break the fence and cause the signals to fall to 'danger'.

The line climbs through wild though green country, past Dalmally and through Taynuilt. We glimpse the Connel Ferry bridge that is now road only but which used to carry the single track of the Ballachulish branch line. Then the line drops round a wide, steep curve to arrive at Oban, the largest fishing port on the west coast north of the Clyde.

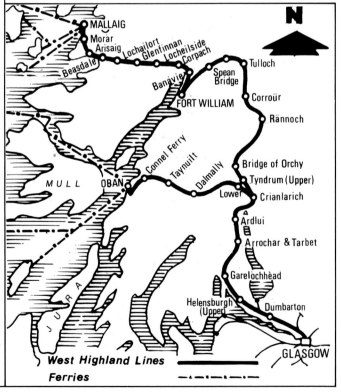

West Highland Lines ——————
Ferries ·—·—·—·—·—

Since dieselisation in 1961 the staple motive power for the West Highland lines for nearly 20 years was the Class 27 BRCW/Sulzer Bo-Bo Type 2. Based on Eastfield depot, these light machines covered all passenger and virtually all freight, with the exception of the occasional English Electric Class 20 and an '08' shunter at Fort William. Sometimes Class 25s appeared but the long climbs did not suit their traction motors. The '27s', and their Class 26 sisters in the far north, became synonymous with the highlands, and their characteristic methodically slow exhausts raised familiar echoes among the mountains.

By the late 1970s it was clear that new efforts were necessary if the passenger traffic was even to keep pace against competition from the steadily improving roads: the bus was nearly an hour faster from Glasgow to Fort William. The problem was that most larger locomotives were too heavy for the lightly constructed track and bridges on these lines – even the similar Class 33s of the Southern Region were too heavy in certain axle weights. However, after judicious easing of the worst curves and some attention to bridges it proved possible to open the West Highland lines to Class 37s, Britain's lightest mixed traffic Co-Cos. With six traction motors and an extra 500hp these machines have permitted considerable speeding up of passenger services and there is now a sense of urgency about this railway that was lacking before.

Eastfield depot rose to the enthusiasm prompted by this improvement, and developed a West Highland terrier motif to identify the '37s' which were intended to be dedicated to these routes. Five of them received names after lochs, and some were decorated with a white line which considerably improved their rather dumpy appearance.

In mid-1981 the author, then Scottish Region's rolling stock engineer, was approached by the operating officer with a request to fit temporary public address equipment on a set of Mk 2 coaches which were wanted to form a Sunday excursion from Edinburgh to Oban. So temporary was the equipment to be, that it had to be removed again in time for Monday's ordinary service! To the suggestion that an air-conditioned push-pull set already so fitted be used, the operating officer explained, 'We don't have any ETH (electric train supply) locomotives of RA5!' (RA5 is the route availability for the West Highland lines.) The author challenged this by exclaiming that the 'Deltics' were RA5, delivered ETH, had the same bogies and motors as the '37s' and were in fact lighter! And wouldn't *Argyll & Sutherland Highlander* be the appropriate one to choose? 55.021 did indeed haul two such excursions to Oban, fully booked as it turned out, the second one being strengthened to eight coaches with a buffet car included. A scenic and historical commentary was provided en route with some interspersed background music.

By the next year the 'Deltics' had gone from BR and the next suggestion, an InterCity 125 set, could not be spared, so the excursions did not run. But the seeds were sown, and the next spur to get ETH working on the West Highland was looming – the demise of the Mk 1 sleeping cars.

At this stage the marketing strength of the Scottish Region management team was beginning to assert itself. While the BRHQ view was that the West Highland sleeping cars should be withdrawn, ScR wanted to project the new Mk 3 sleepers to Fort William. The problem of how to provide an ETH supply quickly and cheaply was solved in original fashion. Three redundant Class 25 locomotives were acquired, their traction motors removed and

their control circuitry modified so that, with the engine running at constant speed, the main generator output could be fixed at 850V dc, the supply being fed via the traction motor contacts to new jumper cables at each end. These vehicles were to be used in effect as generator vans. They cost a fraction of what a freight van conversion would have done using an industrial diesel-alternator set. The work was undertaken at Aberdeen Ferryhill depot; the vehicles were repainted there so as to match the coaches they would be working with, and they were named *ETHEL 1*, *ETHEL 2* and *ETHEL 3*. (ETHEL = ETH Ex Locomotive!) The first trial was on a special working on the Kyle line, followed by the summer Edinburgh-Oban Sunday excursions of 1983.

The next step was to get the Mk 3 sleeping cars to Scotland to connect with the West Highland line. By that summer the Euston-Inverness sleeping car train which previously conveyed the Fort William cars had become air-braked and could not longer carry vacuum-braked sleepers. ScR accepted that to maintain service continuity to Fort William until the Mk 3s became available in October it had to hang the recalcitrant Mk 1s on the back of the Euston-Stranraer train and work the Fort William portion north from Carlisle as a separate train.

The plan from October 1983 was to split the Mk 3s off the Inverness train at Mossend yard, haul them round to Glasgow Queen Street, and drop a Class 37+ETHEL formation on to them with air-braked day stock to form the 05.50 to Fort William. In the event, the operation proved successful and the sleeping car business has kept up reasonably well. The '37'+ETHEL+seven coaches snaking among the mountains in the early morning or evening sunshine make a fine sight, and have brought a touch of quality to the route. The other West Highland trains still required steam heating, and Mk 1 stock is all that could be spared. Conversions of Class 37s to deliver ETH are bringing an end to steam heat here, and probably on BR.

That it has taken so long to explain all this perhaps indicates the disproportionate amount of management time that these peripheral routes take up in relation to the revenue they bring in! Their income is barely a third of their direct costs, a ratio that has spelt closure elsewhere; their survival is entirely due to social, political and strategic necessity.

Having secured the lines' future for the time being in the post-Serpell era, the ScotRail has set out to gain extra revenue from tourists in this most attractive land. The idea of running steam trains on the Mallaig extension line was greeted with scepticism. After all, it was so far from centres of population that there would not be a sufficient market, some said. However, this initiative was published in the public timetable for summer 1984 and was an instant success. It produced a surplus over its direct costs, even allowing for claims for fire damage in the hot 1984 summer, and caused hundreds of additional journeys to be made to the highlands from places all over the UK, so adding to the overall cash receipts of BR.

The idea was developed at business group meetings held by the Area Manager, Fort William. As part of ScR's drive to make its management more business-orientated, each area manager chairs a business group that includes all departments involved in marketing, operating and engineering the railway in his patch. Local initiatives are encouraged provided they have a chance of success. Fort William's extended use of saloons, and now steam locomotives, are small examples in spirit of the initiatives that are beginning to happen all over the rest of the Region.

Left:
The 05.50 from Glasgow Queen Street to Fort William, which conveys sleeping cars from Euston, heads upgrade towards Crianlarich behind No 37.012 *Loch Rannoch* with train heat vehicle No 97.251 *ETHEL 2* in tow, on 28 May 1984.
Mrs Mary Boocock

Below left:
Single line tablets are exchanged as the 08.00 from Oban to Glasgow Queen Street enters Ardlui behind No 37.011 on 21 October 1983.

Above right:
The 18.20 from Glasgow to Oban runs through wild scenery on the climb to Crianlarich behind No 37.188. *Mrs Mary Boocock*

Right:
No 37.012 plus *ETHEL 2* leave Tyndrum Upper with the 05.50 from Queen Street to Fort William on 28 May 1984.

Below:
Under the massive backdrop of Ben Nevis No 37.026 pulls away from Locheilside on 28 May 1984 with the 10.09 from Fort William to Mallaig.

Above:
No 37.264 displays its new livery to admirers at Glenfinnan in May 1984 while working the 14.09 from Fort William to Mallaig.

Left:
The rocky coast just south of Mallaig supports No 37.022 as it leaves with the 15.50 to Fort William on 29 May 1984.
Peter J. C. Skelton

Below left:
Tourist saloon coach No Sc1999 was named *Lochaber* in a short ceremony at Fort William on 8 May 1980.

The Changing Face of

ScotRail

Big enough to manage, small enough to care, motivated enough to succeed – that's ScotRail, the Scottish Region of British Rail

ScotRail is unique. No other Region of British Rail compares. ScotRail's 1,700 route miles include the biggest suburban rail network – Strathclyde – outside of London and, not one, but two of the world's most outstandingly scenic railway lines, the famous West Highland Line (Glasgow to Oban or Mallaig) and the incomparable line to Skye (Inverness to Kyle of Lochalsh), the first in the world equipped with the unique radio signalling system pioneered by British Rail.

ScotRail's 287 passenger stations include 10 which have been opened or reopened since 1983 when the Scottish Region rallied under the 'ScotRail' banner and a new management team to recover lost ground in what is acknowledged to be the most fiercely competitive travel market place in the UK.

Since 1983 stations such as Glasgow (Central and Queen Street), Edinburgh (Waverley and Haymarket), Aberdeen, Arbroath, Dundee, Inverness, Linlithgow, Polmont and Stirling have been restored and modernised. Stranraer now has 'space age' covered walkways, Montrose has a new award-winning station building, and Oban now boasts a similar new building. Among the new, unmanned stations which have opened, the most successful (with 340,000 passenger journeys a year) is Dyce; the most attractive is Bridge of Allan; the most charming is Dunrobin; and the least expensive was Locheil (Outward Bound) which was built by students at the Outward Bound School under ScotRail supervision and without charge.

ScotRail runs more than 1,500 passenger trains daily, earning £96 million from 53 million passenger journeys a year. Freight and parcels revenues are £40 million and £15 million respectively.

A host of improvements in timetable, journey times, catering facilities (including on-train trolley services on certain routes), passenger and enquiry services have been introduced to demonstrate ScotRail's determination to run a highly productive, cost effective railway providing a progressively better standard of customer care. Communications are being steadily improved and highly efficient telephone enquiry bureaux have been established in five key centres. All staff in direct contact with passengers have had at least one session at a 'charm school' with more to follow.

ScotRail has clearly established for itself a distinctive corporate identity based on the unambiguous ScotRail ethos of enterprise, initiative and effort to achieve the slogan it has adopted 'We're getting there . . . Faster'.

Speed, safety, comfort and convenience make

travel the top choice

Overleaf:
The old and new combine to present a vivid contrast of today's ScotRail scene. A modern InterCity 125 express train, flagship of the Aberdeen-London East Coast main line service, passes Dalmeny station, with the world famous Forth Rail Bridge providing an impressive backdrop.

Above:
One of the fast frequent InterCity 125 trains which run between major Scottish centres linking them with principal towns and cities throughout the railway network. Its comfortable air conditioned coaches smooth the miles away on long distance journeys.
Peter J. Robinson

Left:
A Class 86 locomotive hauls a north-bound express on the electrified West Coast main line route. ScotRail has shrunk journey times to London, North-West England, the Midlands and South Wales by raising the top speeds to 110mph on sections of track between Glasgow and the border at Carlisle.

Facing Page:
Trolley catering service is an innovative feature on selected ScotRail services. Introduced on the busy Edinburgh-Glasgow route, it has been expanded to operate on some Strathclyde suburban services and Glasgow-Ayr-Stranraer trains. Smartly dressed staff add to the importance of customer care by providing snacks on the track.

New 'Sprinter' diesel trains are to be progressively introduced on to ScotRail routes and will eventually supersede all existing diesel multiple-units. They are cheaper to run, require less maintenance and are more reliable than the old vehicles which they will replace.

Railfreight handles more than 65,000 cars a year at ScotRail's Bathgate terminal. The movement of bulk quantities like this by rail helps maintain a good environmental balance by using trains for the trunk haul and road for the shorter distances to and from the railhead.

Just over a seventh of ScotRail's total route mileage is electrified. This will be substantially increased with the completion of the Paisley-Ayr route in 1986 and extension to Largs in 1987. Electric multiple-unit trains like this work in the Strathclyde region which boasts the most extensive network of suburban services outside London and South-East England.

Rural lines in Scotland have been upgraded in a drive by ScotRail to increase business and reduce costs. The introduction of converted locomotives and new signalling techniques on single line routes has helped fight coach competition in the scenic but sparsely populated parts of the country.
W. A. Sharman.

Departure/Arrival

Improved stations and increased customer care are among the notable features of ScotRail's determined drive to provide better facilities and higher standards of service for travellers.

Upper Left:
Dundee station is a fine example of how the major passenger terminals have been transformed. It now sports a distinctive house style incorporating the ScotRail theme.

Modernised in a £500,000 scheme, it houses a smart new travel centre able to offer the full range of travel facilities, a new waiting hall, a new travel information indicator, enlarged telephone enquiry bureau and improved toilets including facilities for the disabled. The appearance of the station at both street and platform level is greatly enhanced with terrazzo white floor tiling and stonecleaned retaining walls. Reflective glass panelling gives the building a striking external appearance.

Inset:
TV monitors located at strategic points in stations display a wide range of train and travel information to help passengers.

Lower Left:
Many of ScotRail's busy intermediate stations such as Arbroath, Montrose, Linlithgow, Dumfries, Polmont

and Stirling (pictured here) have been totally refurbished. With new travel centres, better lighting, upgraded train information systems, white tiling, smart functional furniture and eye catching livery, they have vastly improved the image of ScotRail in today's highly competitive transport market.

Right:
Customer care is a prime concern for ScotRail. All staff who come into direct contact with the public are given professional training and those providing back-up support services are set demanding targets for important items like punctuality and carriage cleaning.

Below:
This panoramic view of the concourse at Glasgow Central epitomises the changing face of ScotRail. Gone are the old fashioned stations, outlook and outdated methods of working. In its place new terminals, new equipment, new ideas and a new wave of confidence is sweeping ScotRail through the 1980s, into the 1990s and beyond to the 21st century.

ScotRail
Serves the Nation

ScotRail fulfils a vital role in the transport needs of a nation. It provides the important arteries and support services that carry people and convey freight. Both are essential to maintain economic stability and sustain business expansion.

A large scale investment programme has brought about major improvements, changing the face of ScotRail which – with a staff of more than 15,500 and turnover of some £350 million – is one of the largest industries in the country.

Above left:
The second saloon coach for the West Highland line since the recent revival was No Sc1998, here having its finishing touches applied at Cowlairs depot on 27 May 1983.

Above:
Boats and fishing are the trade marks of Mallaig. No 27.016 waits to leave with the 12.52 to Fort William on 26 May 1980.
Peter Harris

Left:
Steam has brought relative prosperity to the Mallaig extension line in the summer. Class 5 No 5407 was photographed on 28 May 1984 crossing Glenfinnan viaduct with the 11.10 from Fort William.
Mrs Mary Boocock

8
Northern Climbs

Approximately 160 miles beyond Inverness lie the twin terminal towns of Wick and Thurso, and 82 miles west lies Kyle of Lochalsh. There are strong similarities between the railways of the far north and the West Highland lines.

A popular touring route takes the traveller arriving at Mallaig, by ship across to Skye, bus along the island, and back across on the vehicle ferry to rejoin the mainland at Kyle of Lochalsh. Here again stands the familiar Class 37 and steam-heated Mk 1 coaching stock, and again the line strikes out past lochs, rocks and mountains. An old saloon carriage, Great Western or Caledonian, gives the tourists their fill of the steward's tales. And again the summit is on moorland, near Achnasheen – here, in the former, more opulent days of steam, restaurant cars were switched from down to up trains. More mountains surround the train near Garve, the location favoured by a consortium which hopes to build a Swiss-style mountain railway near here, from Strathpeffer to Ben Wyvis. On approaching Dingwall there is a junction with the other single track, the line from Wick and Thurso. Inverness station is reached by an unusual movement in which the train passes by the station on the north side of the triangle, and then reverses into the platform, so that the locomotive and stock can be easily released.

While the Kyle line is the better-known, the route to the far north deserves wider interest. Striking north from Dingwall it runs along the north coastal strip of Cromarty firth and calls at the industrial town of Invergordon. It later turns sharp west to call at the attractive stone town of Tain. Then the train runs along the wooded south shore of Dornoch firth and climbs and turns northwest across a bridge over the valley in full sight of a superbly turretted hillside mansion near Invershin.

Heading inland now the Class 37 climbs hard up into the Sutherland hills. Lairg has sidings for the regular oil tank trains which supply the northern peninsular's needs for fuel oils. The hilly countryside around here has a rolling, rocky but warm quality, the attractive combination of browns, purples and dark greens being unique in the area.

The line, single all the way with passing loops at the several wayside stations, now turns east again, and regains the North Sea coast to call at the small seaside towns of Golspie and Brora. Passing lovely clean, empty, sandy beaches, it soon turns inland again at Helmsdale.

Here begins, in the author's opinion, the wildest stretch of railway in the United Kingdom. We head up a wide, shallow valley, the land becoming gradually featureless. Soon we clickety-clack across heather-covered moorland, a lonely road providing the only sign of civilisation. Many miles later we call at

Below:
On 23 January 1980 the 10.30 to
Kyle of Lochalsh leaves Inverness
behind No 26.040.
Brian Morrison

an oasis in this wilderness: Forsinard station has an hotel nearby, a few trees and a handful of houses for company. Then, veering northeast, we climb into even more desolate land, and pass through a shallow cutting or two. After nearly 30 miles of wilderness we call at a small halt named Altnabreac which delivers little custom. A few miles further on a town appears – and passes by! Halkirk apparently prefers its road link to the coast. The countryside is greener now as we approach Caithness's railway focal point, Georgemas Junction.

The train splits here: after doing business at the platform we draw forward, the Thurso portion is uncoupled from our rear while another Class 37 or a '26' backs on to what was its rear, ready to head north to Thurso. Our front portion heads east across good farmland to Wick on the east coast. This small fishing town is a pleasantly quiet spot. Its one-platform station boasts an unpretentious overall roof that protects the locomotive and perhaps one coach. This is the end of the line, 743 miles from London Euston and 938 from Penzance.

Had we elected instead to join the rear portion from Georgemas we would have found more carriages and passengers with a wish to cover the shorter leg, to Thurso, this time on the north coast. Thurso is a medium-sized market town and harbour and is the hub of the population in these northern extremes. Although it is the northernmost mainland township, it is not as far north as we can go. Across the somewhat unfriendly sea can be seen the Orkney Isles, wide, high and, to me, not very inviting. To the west runs the main, indeed the only, coast road. How many Englanders know that Britain has a *north* coast, with some of the finest, cleanest beaches of all? A few miles along the coast is Dounreay nuclear power station, and beyond that a strange world of ancient rockland, among the oldest emerged rocks in the world, that stretches to Cape Wrath, the barely-accessible northwest tip of our gracious land. But I digress!

Thurso also has a one-platform, overall-roof station. Again there is no locomotive or carriage shed, no fuel point, no mechanical or electrical fitting staff. There is one examiner (now called a rolling stock technician), the only person for over 100 miles who can deal with faults and failures. The spirit in these parts is positive and co-operative, and performance on this long and thin railway remarkably good.

Because of its length and in particular its propensity to wide swings of direction, the railway to the far north has not been fully competitive with road. Scottish Region has imaginatively tackled this by replacing 1,160hp Class 26s with 1,750hp Class 37 diesels, easing speed restrictions and modernising level crossings so that speeds can be raised. Around half an hour has been cut from passenger timings by these means, and the 161 miles from Inverness to Wick now take four hours. Train names being popular again, 'The Orcadian' has reappeared on this line, and 'The Hebridean' runs on the Kyle line. Yet again, steam heating has survived in a northerly area that could be said to be totally unsuitable for a heating medium that can freeze! Electric train heat awaits the delivery of further Class 37/4 locomotives with ETH alternators.

Life has not always been quiet in these afar-off parts. Memories are still fresh of the appalling 1981/82 winter in which the evening train from Inverness to Wick and Thurso left Forsinard in a raging blizzard. As it crossed the northern wilderness beyond, the Class 26 locomotive ploughed into a snowdrift in a cutting. The train crew, determined to get through if they could, backed their train a short distance to take a run at the drift. The snow was filling in behind the train so fast that three coaches were derailed by this

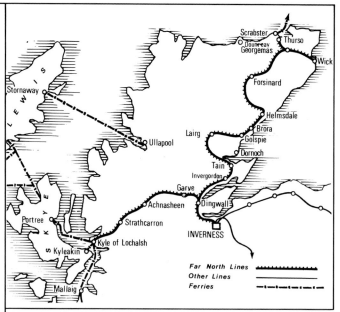

manoeuvre. The locomotive and first coach were detached and run forward at the drift again, but there was to be no escape and the locomotive stuck fast. The crew and passengers settled in the front of the train for the long wait for rescue. The telegraph pole route was down in places, and so communications had been cut and no-one knew where the train was.

Because of the 'white-out' conditions, rescuers waited until daylight next day to search by helicopter for the lost train. Conditions on the train after the train heat boiler water ran out that night can well be imagined. The railway was closed for a week until it could be cleared of snow and derailed vehicles so that normal working could be resumed.

Many lessons were learned from that experience. Firstly, as such a blizzard could be expected any winter, it was decided to equip all Highland, West Highland and far north trains with survival hampers in the guards' vans. These have proved very welcome on several occasions since. Their contents include Mars bars, hot drink kits and other instant, non-perishable foods, and have since had flares added. Another train recently lost in a 'white-out' in broad daylight could have been located quicker by the searching helicopters had flares been used.

Secondly, the loss of a pole route of telecommunication cables not only prevented the flow of information, it cut the basic signal bell-code link between signalboxes. As an emergency replacement, train-to-base radio equipment was set up. Now, signalling north and west of Dingwall is controlled by radio links using electronics to interface between the coded radio signals and otherwise conventional block signalling equipment. Radio links between the Dingwall control centre and the locomotive driving cabs ensure that any incident can be dealt with quickly – no longer does a driver's assistant have to trudge miles to reach a telephone when help is needed. The radio system adopted owes much to the pioneering work of the Ravenglass & Eskdale Railway.

A third advance has been the purchase of a Beilhack snow-blower from West Germany. This is based at Inverness depot and uses rotating blades to cut a path through snowdrifts blocking the line. It came into its own during the snows of the 1983/84 winter and proved its ability to throw the snow well clear of the railway.

A local identity has been developed for the Kyle and Wick/Thurso routes. Locomotives are being reliveried, and embellished with a bold emblem of a black stag's head on a yellow background, inscribed, quite appropriately 'Highland Rail'.

Interest in shortening the route to Wick and Thurso has recently been aroused by a proposal to build a road bridge across the Dornoch firth, if the railway can also use the bridge. The line would, after calling at Tain, strike across the firth on the bridge, run on a short new alignment to the Sutherland county town of Dornoch, and then take up the route of the former Dornoch branch line. It would then leave the branch towards its northern end to regain the present route before Golspie. Time will tell whether financial sponsorship can be obtained for this ambitious scheme.

Above:
The Kyle line is one of the most beautiful in Scotland. Class 26 No 5342 was photographed alongside Loch Luichart on 19 May 1973 with the 17.50 from Inverness. *J. H. Cooper-Smith*

Left:
The welcoming concourse at Inverness station in 1984. Note the terrazzo floor tiles, hanging flower baskets, information kiosk, micro-dot train indicator and the absence of ticket barriers.

Top:
No 37.183 with the 17.35 from Inverness to Wick and Thurso leaves Dingwall on 15 June 1984. The line to Kyle of Lochalsh is in the foreground. *Tom Noble*

Above:
No 26.021 passes time between moves at Georgemas Junction while acting as the Thurso branch engine on 30 May 1977. *Brian Morrison*

Left:
On 12 July 1984 the 06.35 from Inverness to Wick had been reduced to a BG, buffet and TSO when it was photographed leaving Georgemas Junction behind No 37.260 *Radio Highland*. The locomotive's name commemorates the use of radio block signalling on the far north routes. *Tom Noble*

Left:
The notice near the base of the
signal advises the driver of No
37.260 to 'change radio channel'
as he waits for No 26.041 to arrive
at Achnasheen with the 11.10
from Kyle of Lochalsh on 10
August 1983.
A. J. Woof

Above:
The radio console in the cab of a
Class 37 in use on the Kyle line.
Tom Noble

Below:
The small, single platform station
at Britain's most northerly town
boasts an overall roof, not long
enough for the train! No 26.026
has arrived at Thurso with a train
from Inverness in September
1979. *Peter Harris*

9
The ScotRail Fleet

'Second-hand rolling stock.' 'Clapped out buggies.' So ran the style of newspaper comments in the mid and late 1970s when the subject of Scottish Region traction and rolling stock was raised. True, the current age profile is sharply skewed towards the old and well-tried, but today the media is generally less scathing. So why is it that the fleet, which is older now than it was then, attracts less acid criticism?

That the fleet is not so young is clear from the accompanying table (the ages of the locomotives differs little from those of BR as a whole). Backbones of the diesel fleet are the Brush/Sulzer 2,580hp Class 47s and the English Electric 1,750hp Class 37s. These two types of Co-Co handle virtually all diesel locomotive-hauled passenger services within the Region as well as much of the heavier freight. They represent a swing away from the small-engine policy of earlier years when the heaviest passenger trains were regularly double-headed by pairs of Sulzer Type 2 Bo-Bos. Surely no railway in Britain has *ever* has such useful locomotives in its fleet as the '47s'. They are just as much at home hauling 1,500-tonne oil trains at 55mph as they are on passenger trains at up to 95mph.

A further swing has been the efforts in recent years to bring ETH-fitted Class 47/4s into the Region so that a start could be made at eliminating steam heating. Ten years ago, apart from Anglo-Scottish day trains, only the Edinburgh-Glasgow push-pulls had electric train heat (ETH). Now, steam heat has been cleared off the main lines, and is about to be eroded from the peripheral routes as Class 37/4s begin to appear.

The '37/4' results from a BR business decision that extending the life of the Class 37 by up to 20 years represents good value for money. On this class, the locomotive's dc traction generator is replaced by a new alternator with solid state rectification. The addition of an ETH output to this design is thereby made a much easier and lower cost option. The locomotive itself receives a heavy general overhaul which results in a more reliable machine, well suited to its further life span.

The principle of heavy general repairs has been used previously on other ScR types. All '47/4s' are undergoing this work, and the '47/7s', push-pull fitted, were so treated on conversion, having the best utilisation record of any group of '47s' in Britain as a consequence. The Class 47/7s' top speed was raised to 100mph in 1984. Even some of the older Class 26 and 27 Bo-Bos have had to have heavy general overhauls to prolong their lives and enable Class 25s to be eliminated from Scotland.

Mention of the elimination of Class 25 from Scotland reminds one that the erstwhile, if latterly expensive to maintain, Class 40 2,000hp 1Co-Co1s left Scotland finally in 1981.

Above:
The new ScotRail colours grace
No 47.702 *Saint Cuthbert* as it
arrives at Glasgow Central with a
Sunday portion from Edinburgh
of a combined service to Bristol
on 24 February 1985.

The number of Class 20 English Electric Type 1 1,000hp Bo-Bos on the Region has expanded rapidly in recent years as the freight business has begun to appreciate that the eight traction motors and driving axles of a pair of '20s' make a first-rate heavy freight haulage machine. Certainly two Class 20s can move a heavier train than one brand new Class 58 can, albeit at a lower balancing speed. In consequence nearly all Scottish Region's merry-go-round freight trains are hauled by two '20s' fitted for slow-speed crawl.

Updating of locomotives has progressed with the fitting of Classes 20, 26 and 27 for air-brake working so that they can handle freight trains of the modern era.

The technical rejuvenation of the locomotive fleet has been paralleled by visual improvements on some of those which see passenger service. Public interest is sustained by the revived practice of naming locomotives and painting them in attractive liveries. The '47/7s' started with light grey roofs, the last two also being further decked out in the bold style with all-yellow cab-sides, black cab window surrounds and large number and BR symbols. This style has spread to Class 37s used on the West Highland and far north routes. A completely new livery is now appearing on Class 47/4s and 47/7s, based on the new InterCity two-tone grey but with the red stripe replaced by a 'Scottish' blue one, and the locomotives are being labelled 'ScotRail'.

Likewise the ageing diesel multiple-unit fleet presents a better image nowadays than it did when the author first worked on the Region in 1976. Gone is the drab, all-over rail blue livery. Gone also is the miserable grey seat moquette that stained black with wear and washing. All sets have been repainted blue-and-grey, and all see carriage washing machines more frequently than before. Indeed, DMUs based at Ayr are receiving the striking Strathclyde red livery, and local initiative has had them running with brightly cleaned silver buffers!

Internally, almost all ScR DMUs have been refurbished with fluorescent lighting, brighter decor, quieter engine mountings and repositioned heater air-intakes, and present a more satisfactory image than previously. The Class 107s also received new Leyland 680/1595 engines. As mentioned elsewhere, there are three main classes of DMU: the standard Class 101 Metro-Cammell; and two Derby types, the medium-density Class 107 and the high-density Class 116. However, following a serious fire at Ayr depot in January 1984 when seven DMU cars were badly damaged, the Region has had to import BRCW Class 104s from the Manchester area, a type not previously seen in Scotland. These have been integrated into Ayr's fleet, have been put through works overhaul, and they look smart in blue-and-grey.

Future policy is to replace the existing DMUs with new Class 150-series diesel multiple-units, initially in the Edinburgh suburban group of services. Eventually it is hoped these will be available in sufficient number to cover all Scottish internal diesel passenger routes with the exception of the main lines. The greater carrying capacity and higher availability of the Class 150 breed will enable the total number of vehicles for a given service to be reduced.

Mention has already been made of the Region's three classes of electric multiple-units in the Strathclyde chapter. The Region is fortunate that each build of EMUs it has received since 1959 has been to a very up-to-date design. The next group will be the Class 318s for the Ayrshire electrification scheme. These will be based on the standard Class 317 unit familiar on the St Pancras-Bedford route, except that they will be three-car sets, will have the latest front end as used on Class 455 on the Southern Region from late

Table 1
Scottish Fleet Age Profile – 1985

Type	No in fleet	Average age (years)
Diesel main line locomotives	277	22
Electric locomotives (Class 81)	19	25
Electric multiple-units (sets)	106	21
Diesel multiple-units (sets)	86	27
Coaching stock:		
passenger	457	21
non-passenger	53	27
High Speed Train sets (2+8)	5	6

Table 2
ScotRail Fleet – 1 January 1985

Type	Class	No in fleet	Totals
Diesel locomotives	47	62	
	37	66	
	27	50	
	26	33	
	20	66	
		Total	277
Shunting locomotives	08		64
Electric locomotives	81		19
HST power cars	43		10
HST trailer cars	Mk 3		41
APT power cars	49		2
APT trailer cars			11
Electric multiple-units	303	71	
(three-car seats)	311	19	
	314	16	
		Total	106
Diesel multiple-units	101	51	
(three-car seats)	104	3	
	107	23	
	116	9	
		Total	86
Coaching stock	Mk 1	147	
	Mk 2	249	
	Mk 3a	32	
	Sleep	20	
	Catg	9	
		Total	457
Non-passenger-stock	BG		53

1984, will have toilets and outer suburban seating, and presumably will be resplendent in Strathclyde red livery.

Scottish Region operates coaching stock of almost every type on BR. Its stars are the 34 Mk 3a coaches used on the Edinburgh-Glasgow push-pulls, which are now being outshopped in the new ScotRail livery, two-tone grey with blue-and-white stripes, to match the '47/7s'. Next down the scale are the Mk 2d and 2f air-conditioned stock which works on services north to Aberdeen. Another group of around 95 Mk 2ds, 2es and 2fs is based at Polmadie and has integrated workings as far afield as Aberdeen, Plymouth, Cardiff, Harwich, Liverpool, Manchester and Bournemouth. These are the only Scottish coaches normally to be seen south of the border.

Pressure-ventilated Mk 2a, 2b and 2c coaches cover the Glasgow and Edinburgh to Inverness services, and act as seating coaches on certain Anglo-Scottish overnight trains. Forming a further Mk 2 group are the vacuum-braked sets which work on the Edinburgh-Dundee semi-fasts and on the Inverness-Aberdeen route. Because of their already dating interior style, these have been brightened up by painting the entrance cross-vestibules a welcoming bright yellow. All retain blue-and-grey livery and now carry the ScotRail legend.

The Mk 1s have been a problem for some years. Ten years ago many had been allowed to run down in the belief that they were to be replaced: their internal appearance did the Region no justice at all. Efforts were made to retrim their seating with the then standard blue-green check moquette, and the open saloons received blue melamine table tops to replace the drab and often peeling black rexine. These actions restored appearances until the turn of the decade when the scrapping of vehicles still bearing asbestos insulation caused their wholesale replacement by coaches from other Regions. This brought back on to the Region the compartmented SK type. Previously, open TSO stock had been preferred in Scotland for its greater seating capacity, its suitability for observation on scenic routes, and the fact that vandalism tends to be higher on compartment stock.

Dissatisfaction with the dated image projected by these old vehicles led the Region unilaterally to adopt BR's cheapest face-lifting programme. The dim 'goldfish-bowl' lighting in the TSOs was replaced by easily wired-in square fluorescent units. The stained interior woodwork below windows was painted matt black as were other easily damaged areas such as seat ends, and the entrance cross-vestibules were painted a welcoming light yellow. The SKs had their compartment lighting replaced by two short fluorescent tubes following recent Western Region practice, and system maps were placed in strategic locations, a useful aid for the many tourists who fequently turn to them for guidance.

It had been BRHQ's intention that all Mk 3a sleeping cars should be maintained at the two large depots in London, Willesden and Bounds Green. However, it proved difficult to diagram the sleeping cars on the Scotland-Bristol route to these points and so this batch is based at Craigentinny, Edinburgh. In addition, the four cars used on the Glasgow and Edinburgh to Inverness overnight trains are also based there. Craigentinny is the base for the five InterCity 125 sets owned by the Scottish Region and used as part of the East Coast main line fleet. Therefore the only significant group of locomotive-hauled passenger stock on BR that is not represented in the ScR fleet is the Mk 3a catering car, although these appear nightly at Polmadie off the West Coast main line.

Future changes in the fleet are not clear at this stage, though at the time of writing the Region's aspirations are. ScR aims for its internal diesel passenger routes to be covered by only two types of traction, HST sets cascaded to the internal main lines following East Coast main line electrification, and 150-series DMUs on all other non-electrified routes. This would revolutionise the image of Scotland's rail services and provide passengers with something that offers good competition with anything the bus operators can provide.

As a result of the accident at Polmont in which a push-pull train was derailed when it hit a cow that had strayed on to the line, the driving trailers were fitted in 1985 with impact deflectors (ie, cow-catchers). They are the first BR vehicles to be so fitted. The decision arose from concern expressed following the public enquiry, that a train with the locomotive at the rear and running at 100mph speeds might have a higher propensity to derail on impact with a large obstruction.

Below:
Royalty has a long tradition in Edinburgh! No 47.541 was named *The Queen Mother* in 1982, and is seen here standing awaiting departure with the 13.20 to Inverness on 30 October 1982.

Above:
Five HST sets are allocated to the Scottish Region for East Coast main line services. One such passes Cowlairs while working the 08.00 from Edinburgh to Glasgow prior to returning with the daily through service to London King's Cross.

Left:
Only one Class 27 received the white stripe treatment, No 27.056. *Tim Boocock*

Below left:
When availability of '47/7s' and driving trailers became sufficiently good, an additional push-pull set was made up using Mk 2 coaches; it is seen here at Waverley.

Top right:
The neat outline of a Glasgow EMU is evident from this view of No 311.104 crossing the Clyde bridge on the approach to Glasgow Central with a service from Neilston on 21 June 1983. *Tim Boocock*

Centre right:
Strathclyde red (or is it orange?) looks excellent on the modern Class 314 units such as the one seen here on 23 August 1983 at High Street on a service to Dalmuir.

Right:
The new PTE livery has spread to DMUs based at Ayr. No 107.444 passes Howwood on 14 May 1984 on the 11.35 from Glasgow to Ayr. *Tom Noble*

Above:
At one time a Class 25, now *ETHEL 1* No 97.250 is one of three train heat generator vehicles converted by the Scottish Region for use on the West Highland lines.

Left:
Coach No Sc1998 was once a LNER inspection saloon. Restored to the colours of that railway at Cowlairs, the coach was internally refurbished for the 1983 season.

Below left:
Approaching Georgemas Junction on 11 July 1984 is No 37.025 with the 18.00 from Wick to Inverness. *Tom Noble*

Above:
No 37.027 stands at Dundee and displays its new nameplates *Loch Eil*, its highland terrier motif and its Eastfield stripe.

Right:
A stag's head (right) indicates that No 47.461 belongs to Inverness depot . . . while the castle over the nameplate (below right) on No 47.710 professes allocation to Haymarket.

10 Maintaining the Fleet

Did you know that a DMU which works a stopping service from Glasgow Central to Ayr with a clear road and the usual 11 intermediate stops changes from one gear to another at least 60 times? And did you know that for each gear change a minimum of eight electro-pneumatic (EP) valves operate on a standard three-car set? That means that between the Glasgow departure and the arrival at Ayr there have been 480 EP valve operations. In a day a typical set will have upwards of 5,280 EP valve operations, or perhaps 1¼ million operations in a year!

Or take as an example a Class 303 EMU on a typical Glasgow suburban diagram. It will call at around 240 stations in the day. Its 24 sliding doors will have made a total of 5,750 or so operations that day, or approximately 1½ million in a year.

Or take the case of one piston on a Class 47 locomotive. This is likely to make over 60 million reverse strokes in a year! And there are 12 of these on a locomotive!

Confronted with facts like these, the author is never surprised on those occasions when something goes wrong. Indeed one can be pleased that the system works as well as it does when one realises that that locomotive's crankshaft has made more than one thousand million revolutions since it was new! The task of making sure that the equipment works with an acceptable degree of reliability rests squarely on the shoulders of the engineers.

As a rough and ready rule it can be shown that passengers begin to complain about service reliability when the performance of locomotives or units falls significantly below 10,000 miles per casualty (a casualty is any defect which causes the cancellation of a passenger train or a delay of five minutes or more). The Regional Mechanical & Electrical Engineer (RM&EE) in Scotland has four depots which carry out preventive maintenance on diesel main line locomotives, the largest being at Eastfield, Glasgow and at Haymarket near Edinburgh. The Board's Director of Mechanical & Electrical Engineering (DM&EE) lays down strictly-defined specifications of the work that needs to be done to a locomotive or vehicle and at what intervals. The RM&EE fixes the facilities and staffing at the depots to be sufficient to meet this workload plus repairs which arise from examinations and from out-of-course failures.

The difference between a reliable locomotive and an unreliable one so often rests on the degree of adherence to the specifications that is achieved at the depots, and this falls to the area maintenance engineers to ensure. Success comes from good staff training, sufficient and intelligent supervision and above all attention to detail by the skilled workshop staff.

'This place is like a palace – what a difference compared with Orpington!' So exclaimed Sir Peter Parker, then chairman of the

Table 3
ScotRail Depots – 1 January 1985

Maintenance Depots

	Types of stock/work	No allocated
Eastfield	Diesel locomotives	122
	Diesel shunters	9
	Diesel multiple-units	20 sets
Haymarket	Diesel locomotives	85
	Diesel shunters	11
	Diesel multiple-units	25 sets
Inverness	Diesel locomotives	45
	Diesel shunters	3
	Coaching stock	89
	Non-passenger stock	26
	Light wagon repairs	–
Motherwell	Diesel locomotives	26
	Diesel shunters	16
	Wagons	–
Shields	Electric locomotives	19
	Electric multiple-units	35 sets
	Advanced Passenger Train	2
	Overhead line	–
Hyndland	Electric multiple-units	67 sets
Ayr	Diesel multiple-units	41 sets
	Diesel shunters	6
Craigentinny	High Speed Trains	5 sets
	Coaching stock	127
	Non-passenger stock	13
Polmadie	Coaching stock	211
	Non-passenger stock	14
Aberdeen Clayhills	Coaching stock	28
Millerhill	Wagons	–

Servicing Depots (other than those above)

	Purpose	Type of stock	Allocation
Aberdeen Ferryhill	Service	Diesel locos	–
	Maintain	Diesel shunters	4
	Lt repair	Wagons	–
Thornton	Service	DMUs & DLs	–
	Maintain	Diesel shunters	12
Perth (station)	Service	Coaching stock	–
Grangemouth	Service	Diesel locos	–
	Maintain	Diesel shunters	3
Millerhill	Service	Diesel locos	–
Cowlairs	Service	Coaching stock	–
Corkerhill	Service	DLs, DMUs, EMUs	–
Bridgeton	Service	EMUs	–
Townhead (Ayr)	Service	DMUs	–

Other Work Locations

	Department	Purpose
Slateford	Civil Eng	On-track plant overhaul
Motherwell	Civil Eng	Long-welded rail
Rutherglen	Civil Eng	On-track plant mtce
Irvine	S&T Eng	Signal manufacture & repair
Perth (New Yard)	M&E Eng	Light wagon repairs
Falkland Jct (Ayr)	M&E Eng	Light wagon repairs
Carstairs	M&E Eng	Overhead line

Table 3 (continued)

Glasgow Central	M&E Eng	Plant & machinery
Edinburgh New St	M&E Eng	Plant & machinery
Cathcart	M&E Eng	Electric control
ScotRail House	Operating	Regional control
Polmadie	M&E Eng	T&RS repairs

Board, when being shown round the maintenance shed at the depot complex at Craigentinny, Edinburgh. Craigentinny is one of Scotland's newer depots having been re-built in 1979 to maintain InterCity 125 sets and the coaching stock based at Edinburgh.

A high speed train or a Glasgow push-pull arriving at Craigentinny at the end of a day's work first stops on one of two reception and fuelling tracks for the power cars or the locomotive to be serviced. Then it proceeds through the train washing machine, reverses in Portobello sidings and runs on to one of three covered inspection pits in the main shed group. A couple of hours later it is on the move again and is placed on a track in the cleaning shed where the train is prepared cosmetically for the next day's duties. Subsequently it is stabled in an open siding, and connected to an ETH shore supply so that the train can be pre-heated before entering service.

Alongside the inspection shed is a small repair shop which can tackle any repair from changing an HST's turbo-blower or traction motor to a carriage wheel set or air-conditioning equipment module.

The depot's allocation includes the group of Mk 3a sleeping cars which is used on the Bristol service and on the Scottish internal routes to Inverness. As these coaches have retention toilet effluent tanks, a facility for pumped discharge of these has been provided in the depot yard. Other depots' sleepers are similarly discharged on day-time turnround.

In all up to 200 vehicles are received and despatched daily at Craigentinny, most movements taking place in the evening and early morning; activity is highest at night. During the day, work proceeds on the heavier examinations on the maintenance spare HST set and the spare push-pull set. The working of the latter is interesting. All five Mk 3a and the three Mk 2d push-pull sets have intensive operating diagrams which enable them to visit Craigentinny at least once in any eight days. It is a simple matter therefore to rotate them through the maintenance spare set. This enables full maintenance attention to be given on the day shift when the pressures on movements are lower and when full supervisory and management attention can be given to the quality of the product.

The other main carriage maintenance depot is at Polmadie, south of Glasgow Central. This serves the West Coast main line group of train sets. There is a smaller, new depot at Inverness to cover the stock that works in the north of Scotland, and an even smaller one at Aberdeen Clayhills which is there principally to ensure HSTs from the East Coast main line are returned to traffic in good working order.

The two large locomotive depots are at Eastfield and Haymarket. Eastfield, just beyond the top of the bank out of Glasgow Queen Street station, is a tight fit for its allocation of around 120 locomotives and 20 DMU sets; Haymarket, likewise, can get congested if too many DMUs or locomotives arrive for repairs in a short time. A diesel locomotive can receive a wide range of attention, from fuelling only, through a minor inspection in the servicing shed, to a major examination that is programmed to take up to three days. In addition, both these large depots have special equipment for lifting locomotives off their bogies so that wheels or traction motors can be changed, and for cleaning the underframe and bogies of a locomotive in order to eliminate possible dirt concentrations that could in time form a fire risk. In addition, Eastfield has a Hegenscheidt ground wheel lathe that is used for locomotives and DMUs. This is due to be retired after a new one is installed at Craigentinny and the existing one at Shields is renewed.

Control of the fleet has moved a long way since the days of steam. Locomotive depots now use the computerised TOPS network to obtain details of the maintenance status of locomotives and their location. DMUs are not yet on TOPS, but the supervisors at DMU depots such as Eastfield say they would be lost without the small but comprehensive planning board system they have used in the last few years.

In contrast to Inverness's new carriage shed is the locomotive depot there which is housed in what was once the Loch Gorm works of the former Highland Railway company. It is a less appropriate environment for modern day working and the Region is debating whether a case can be made to invest in a better facility, possibly linked to the new carriage shed.

Also housed in a former steam shed is Motherwell's small depot which looks after the Class 37 fleet that services Ravenscraig steel works. This depot building is shared with the wagon shops, now the largest such in Scotland. Originally there was a much larger wagon shop here, in a wide, timber building incorporating a good overhead crane lift facility and wheel and journal lathes. However, the condition of the building led to the decision to rationalise, a feat made possible by the wholesale change in the size and nature of the BR wagon fleet. There was surplus capacity in the 'PPM shop', the other half of the steam shed in which BSC iron ore tipplers, Freightliners and other modern wagons were given planned, preventive maintenance. By the absorption of part of the adjoining traction depot, a cost-effective wagon shop was produced.

The fall in the size of the wagon fleet also led to complete closure in 1983 of the wagon depot at Townhill near Dunfermline, once the largest in the Region. It is a measure of changing times tnat, whereas 10 years ago there were 70 men at Townhill covering wagon repairs, since the depot closure a mobile gang of two men was more than sufficient to meet repairs arising in the Fife area, and even this has now been disbanded.

The largest depot which undertakes multiple-unit maintenance is Shields, west of Glasgow Central, at which is based the south Glasgow electric units. The depot also owns the 18 Class 81 Bo-Bo electric locomotives, the only electric locomotives to be based in Scotland despite its location at the northern end of the West Coast main line. The life-extended Class 303s are being allocated there so that they can be put to work on the Gourock route when driver-only operation is implemented.

The rest of the EMU fleet operates from the north side of the Clyde and the depot there is at Hyndland, in the residential west end of Glasgow. This is the depot built for the purpose when the first lines were electrified in 1960, and looks after two-thirds of the fleet. It has always been predominantly a maintenance depot, the cleaning of the north side EMUs having been done for years at the site of the former terminus station at Bridgeton Central. Since services ceased there in 1979 when the new Bridgeton station was opened on the Argyle line, there has been interest in closing the branch altogether and building a new cleaning depot at Yoker.

Likewise, the south side electric units were cleaned in the open air at Smithy Lye, between Glasgow parcels depot and Shields.

The first stage of the Ayrshire electrification has been to wire to Corkerhill depot so that EMUs can be cleaned in the spacious five-track shed there.

Diesel multiple-units used to be maintained at six locations in Scotland. Introduction of some locomotive-hauled workings has enabled these to be reduced to three. DMUs no longer work from Inverness (but future builds of the new Class 150s may find employment on those lines up there), and the depots at Dundee and Hamilton were closed in 1981 and 1982. One might argue that three depots is still too many for a fleet of around 86 three-car sets, but bear in mind that two of them are shared with locomotives and all are at critical locations in relation to the service pattern, and the system appears to hold good.

Certainly the depot at Ayr has been brought up to a modern standard in the last 10 years. It has been re-roofed, given new pit lighting, new shed lighting, new concrete floor surfaces inside the main shed, good areas for heater repair and battery maintenance, new offices and an extended stores. Its allocated units work very hard with frequent stops and hard running between them on the 'Ayrshire corridor' routes.

At the Glasgow end of the Ayr route is one more depot, of a different kind. Corkerhill has a single track DMU repair shed whose purpose is to ensure that any DMU set that arrives at the depot for cleaning, fuelling or stabling and which also needs some repairs can be repaired in time to take up the next stage of its diagrammed working. Corkerhill does not have a maintenance allocation but it is the central point to which all south side multiple-units come between peaks, and so a repair facility is a must.

Glasgow's industrial heritage at one time included at least five locomotive works. Of these, only that at Saint Rollox remains. It was formerly the Caledonian Railway's principal engineering centre, but now forms British Rail Engineering Ltd's Scottish workshops. As such, it provides a service to the Scottish Region for the heavy overhaul and repair of all its carriages and multiple-units, and those locomotives (Classes 26 and 27) which are peculiar to Scotland.

In anybody's imagination, Glasgow works is a very large operation, employing about 1,500 men. At the time of writing the site is of 42 acres, of which some 16 acres are under cover. The central feature is a set of high-roofed buildings containing the locomotive erecting shop and associated sections, and the wheel shop which produces repaired wheelsets for all types of railway vehicle. Each bay is about 40ft wide and 1,000ft long. Their height is impressive, but essential to the need to use overhead travelling cranes that can lift and move locomotives or their components around the shop. Some of these cranes are each able to lift 60 tons, two together being used when a locomotive requires lifting. A section of one of these bays overhauls Sulzer diesel power units, and another carries out the repair of locomotive bogies.

Adjacent is the carriage works section, lower in roof height but very large in terms of floor area. The dominant and unique feature of this shop is the traverser that crosses the centre of the shop. This performs the normal function of moving carriages around from one track or repair bay to another. But it also carries the lifting jacks on which all carriages and most multiple-units are lifted for their bogies to be removed for overhaul. This eliminates the need for heavy cranes and simplifies the handling of bogies to and from the nearby repair bays.

The carriage works overhauls all types of ScotRail coaches and multiple-units except the Mk 3a sleeping cars and HST sets. The heaviest work undertaken there is the life extension and refurbishing of the Class 303 EMUs. The conversion of 13 Mk 2f BSOs to driving trailers for the Edinburgh-Glasgow and Glasgow-Aberdeen push-pull trains was also a Glasgow works achievement.

Around the main locomotive and carriage works are many complementary facilities. DMU diesel engines, gearboxes and final drives are overhauled here, as are traction motors, main generators and carriage motor-alternators. There is a large trimming shop to handle seat moquette replacement, and the usual machine, fabrication, electrical and fitting shops. And did you know that Glasgow works specialises in making overhead electrification structures? The carriage paint shop is in a separate building fed by an outside traverser. Having tried spray painting in earlier years, BREL works have generally realised that the amount of masking-up that this method requires is not cost-effective. A trial of pressure-fed paint rollers was promising, but in common with other works, Glasgow has come back to using paint brushes. This suits the increasingly complicated vehicle liveries of modern times.

Glasgow works also has an accredited electronic component repair room. This is essential nowadays to support the equipment used in modern EMU control systems, coaching stock air-conditioning, motor-alternator controls and the push-pull equipment on locomotives and driving trailers.

Crewe works specialises in the overhaul of Class 47, 37 and 20 locomotives. The BREL view is that it would be less economic to split this specialisation between more than one location, so Scotland's locomotives of these classes visit Crewe for their scheduled overhauls and for major repairs. In fact the cost of moving locomotives this distance is a minimal proportion of the cost of overhaul, and in many cases the movement can be accomplished by working revenue-earning trains. Thus the new ScotRail colours on Class 47s are becoming known across the Pennines and north of York!

It is less well known among railway enthusiasts that the Region has other depots which produce or maintain equipment for other departments. For example, at Irvine, north of Troon, the Regional Signal & Telegraph Engineer has a workshop which repairs and overhauls signalling equipment. At Slateford, near Edinburgh on the Shotts line, are the Regional Civil Engineer's workshops, recently refurbished to undertake maintenance of on-track machines and cranes. Smaller depots do the day-to-day checking of ballast tampers and other on-track machines: one such is the single vehicle shed at Rutherglen which was built new alongside the West Coast main line only a few years ago. At the time of writing, the Regional Mechanical & Electrical Engineer's new crane overhaul shop is being built at Polmadie, adjacent to the locomotive repair shop there.

Above left:
Scotland's largest rolling stock depot is Craigentinny. In this view of the maintenance shed can be seen an InterCity 125 set (left) and Edinburgh-Glasgow push-pull stock.

Left:
Opened in May 1983, the new carriage maintenance depot at Inverness was built to cater for all Scottish internal stock on services radiating from Inverness.

Above:
Three months after regular use began, the interior of Inverness carriage maintenance shed is seen here to be as immaculate as when it was new!

Right:
A High Speed Train is being serviced in the small inspection shed at Aberdeen Clayhills, photographed at about 01.00 on 4 January 1979.

Below:
Despite its very large allocation of 131 diesel locomotives, Eastfield depot is a compact structure on a site offering insufficient stabling room. The low shed on the right is a fully enclosed fuelling point.
Tom Noble.

Left:
A Class 107 DMU enters the new single road repair shed at Corkerhill, southwest of Glasgow Central, in March 1981.

Below:
Shields depot was Scotland's first really up-to-date maintenance depot building. In this view it houses refurbished EMU No 303.056 and an APT set (right).

Above:
As first built in 1981, Eastfield's fuelling point offered only part shelter. No 37.112 leads an '08' and another Class 37 in the queue for attention.

Above left:
A new carriage washing machine was installed in 1983 at Aberdeen Clayhills.

Above:
A major activity in Glasgow works is the life extension of Class 303 EMUs. This includes complete removal of asbestos body insulation and the cutting out of corroded body members.

Left:
In former times as seen here the wagon shop at Townhill was a hive of activity. It closed on 24 January 1983.

Below left:
Another branch of maintenance is permanent way engineering. In this view of an official inspection in progress, selected sleepers are inspected at Bannockburn, while the sun shines on Stirling castle in the background.

11
Customer First

It may be quite obvious to retailers and others in commerce that the customer must come first if the business is to survive. But why should that not also apply to transport, and more particularly to railways? Traditionally the railway has been kept alive by its advances in technology and operating improvements. When traffic is seen to have dropped, action has been taken to reduce costs, sometimes by cutting services, routes, stations or depots. The cynical may be forgiven for suggesting that it is only in recent years that our railways have become skilful at maximising the revenue obtained from customers by judicious marketing.

One of the problems has always been the gap that exists between the station or area which has day-to-day contact with customers, and the Regional headquarters where traditionally the marketing expertise has been housed. When, in 1983, BR prepared its in-house drive to make railwaymen more customer-aware, the Scottish Region's input to the forming of proposals was much greater than its small size would suggest.

For by then the advantages of its organisation, which had dispensed with the divisional level of management several years before, had begun to lead to very close involvement in customer matters by all relevant departments, including the operating and engineering ones as well as the marketing functions. Several schemes were already under way to improve the Region's image to the passengers.

But Scottish Region includes in its definition of customers such large bodies as Strathclyde PTE and British Steel. The railways' managers have been encouraged to get out into the rough commercial world to make contacts and to sell rail transport as well as to listen to customer needs and bring back into the railway the lessons so learned. Recently the marketing function has been reorganised so that each railway 'business' – InterCity, Provincial, Freight and Parcels – has its own business manager in the Region and can concentrate on his own sector.

The attitudes are gradually being reflected in Scottish Region's hardware. The new ScotRail livery, the facelifting of older rolling stock, really open 'open stations', new road bus links to widen the railway's catchment areas – these are but a few of the fruits of the new era.

On the freight side there has been much hard-won new traffic, most of which has already been referred to in earlier chapters. But the link between marketing and performance has never been so well forged as in the efforts that were made to ensure, for example, that the Petfoods traffic from Paisley to Wisbech ran on time. That firm does not keep intermediate stocks of goods, stocks being equal to money, and so a late train means that another firm's goods are sold from the supermarket shelves. Equally the railway

Above:
Potential rail customers are shown the latest in freight and passenger rolling stock, as well as a glimpse into the past, at an exhibition marking 100 years of Glasgow Central station on 5 August 1979. No 47.555 *The Commonwealth Spirit* leaves on the 12.50 to Euston.

is under very close watch from the Newspaper Proprietors Association and the Post Office, which cannot afford their goods to be delivered late. Late post is not 'first class', and who buys old newspapers?

The art of survival, however, demands that a balance be maintained between the potential for filling seats which lower fares can do, and the temptation to raise fares to raise income. Marketing men are becoming astute at assessing the elasticity of their particular market sectors. This is no constant statistical phenomenon. One can raise fares quite happily in a market where passengers must travel (for example to work) and no other reasonable alternative exists – but try doing this after the 'rules' have been changed and local bus companies are chasing after the same passengers.

That a price war did occur on the Inverness-Wick/Thurso route is quite probable. In that case three bus firms competed with ScotRail for the relatively meagre traffic on offer. Only one bus firm now covers this long distance service and by careful judgement BR held on to its share. In the PTE area the Transcard zonal fare ticket is inter-modal and price changes are made to rail and road at the same time. This keeps their relative competitive positions constant.

On InterCity the aim once was to maximise revenue by pricing up those fares paid by business travellers on expense accounts. The recession changed the elasticity of that market to the point where it diminished sharply. A different market had to be encouraged to travel InterCity, and the proliferation of Saver fares managed to keep revenue fairly buoyant while filling seats.

Nonetheless, the onward drift of cost inflation and the relative difficulty in trying to be original with trains and rolling stock that are not going to change much for some time mean that the margin between costs and income gets worse. Action therefore has to be taken to reduce costs.

The PTE area can be used as an example of typical action and reaction to this type of situation. The recession did cause a small but significant reduction in the number of people travelling. Discussion between BR and the PTE elicited several ways in which costs could be saved. One way would be to reduce the timetable and run fewer, in some cases longer, trains. This might cause further customer resistance because fewer trains means longer waits between them. An alternative, the one adopted, was to run the same number of trains but reduce the number running as six-car formations. This cuts costs less but preserves revenue. In the end the choice is a judgement, arrived at in a professional way. (This particular example had a useful spin-off because the displaced Class 303 units went to the London Midland Region and enabled the older Class 506s to be retired from the Glossop line.)

In the Provincial sector the reduction in DMUs caused by similar pruning actions brought nearer the possibility of making a really large financial saving by the closure of a maintenance depot. Too many DMUs still remained there to be capable of being absorbed in other depots. However, there was spare capacity in the nearby locomotive and carriage depots and so a proposal was evaluated to replace DMUs on one route by locomotives and coaches. Traditional accounting methods suggested that locomotives were normally more expensive than DMUs, but the ability actually to close a depot made this a means to more cost-effective operation.

Taking such a decision is not easy for any manager or engineer: it involves the dislocation of many people from their established working lives, there is sometimes hardship to be faced and overcome, and there is always opposition from local interests which correctly see another source of employment in their area being lost. Nonetheless, the railway's policy of enabling staff who wish to, to move to other railway jobs, and others who prefer to leave to do so under reasonable terms, has facilitated this difficult task. This policy receives the active support of the trades unions.

An important part of projecting the railway's customer appeal is its publicity and public relations. ScotRail has put a high priority on its public affairs activities for many years. It has forged close relationships with Members of Parliament, councillors and opinion formers throughout Scotland. As a result of these contacts the railway has been blessed with financial and other support for many projects, and a greater understanding when firm action has to be taken on costs.

The Region also likes to get its achievements talked about in the media of television and the press. The ScotRail campaign has been very successful in this. Many towns, burghs and cities have been delighted to get on to the InterCity 125 map, and others have responded warmly to the honour of having appropriate names placed on the sides of locomotives or HST power cars.

All the activities in this chapter are master-minded from the Region's single headquarters at ScotRail House (formerly Buchanan House) in Glasgow. Visitors to that building will find there a high activity rate that is not found in many other headquarters of large industries. All departments being in the same building helps to ensure that they work together closely. The past years of getting decisions made through an endless series of meetings, committees and bureaucracy are at an end – well, almost!

Left:
'Can I help you?' ScotRail's first attempt at a hostess point on the concourse at Waverley, in September 1983.

Above right:
Welcome to the new travel centre at Glasgow Central.

Right:
Modern architecture welcomes customers. This awning links BR's Queen Street station with the PTE's Buchanan Street underground station in Glasgow. Only one snag – this entrance is in Dundas Street!

time now **13 32**

← Low Level trains
for Dalmuir, Dumbarton Cent,
Lanark, Milngavie, Motherwell
and intermediate stations
Entrance to Low Level station by
means of escalator next platform 13

13 43
Carstairs
Carlisle, Preston,
Crewe, Wolverhampton
Birmingham (New Street)
Birmingham (International)
Coventry
Leamington Spa
Banbury, Oxford,
Reading
London (Paddington)
Buffet to Wolverhampton

14 10
Carlisle
Preston

Watford (Junction)
London (Euston)

and Buffet Car

13 45
Dunlop
Stewarton
Kilmarnock
Kirkconnel
Dumfries
Annan
Carlisle

D E P A

PLATFORM 1

PLATFORM 2

PLATFORM 3

PLATF

Train services from this station ↓

Left:
The old order in departure
indicators at Glasgow Central was
very clear, but labour intensive
when compared with the
micro-dot edifice at Glasgow
Queen Street. On occasions the
centre screen here displays a
welcoming message in Gaelic!

Departures
Time Destination Plat Calling at
1400 EDINBURGH 2 HAYMARKET
1408 GRAHAMSTON 1 BISHOPBRGG LENZIE CROY
1430 EDINBURGH 2 FALKIRK H HAYMARKET
1438 DUNBLANE 4 BISHOPBRGG LENZIE CROY
LARBERT STIRLING
1500 EDINBURGH 2 HAYMARKET

Special notices
ATTENTION SENIOR CITIZENS.
HOLDERS OF RAILCARDS CAN
TRAVEL ANYWHERE IN SCOTLAND
FOR 2 POUNDS RETURN AND
ANYWHERE IN ENGLAND FOR
2 POUNDS SINGLE. THIS
FANTASTIC OFFER IS OPEN UNTIL
NOV 30 TRAVEL AFTER 0930. WHY
NOT PICK UP A LEAFLET AT THE
TRAVEL CENTRE AND ENJOY
YOURSELVES.

Arrivals
Time Origin Plat
1335 DUNBLANE 1 10
1342 EDINBURGH 2
1350 ABERDEEN 7
1405 GRAHAMSTON 4
1415 EDINBURGH 2
1435 DUNBLANE 1

5

Left:
'Training beats coaching' – a sporty metaphor for ScotRail's slogan, photographed at Edinburgh on 24th January 1985.

Below left:
ScotRail supports Glasgow City's campaign for recognition that the city is a better place.

Below:
This car-borne promotion of ScotRail's cut-price competitive fare to Inverness was parked outside Glasgow's independent coach operators' bus park in May 1983!

Above:
Freight containers for industrial customers are loaded on to a liner train at Glasgow's Gushetfaulds terminal.

Left:
The first consignment of 36in gas mains pipes to be stacked six to a wagon being loaded at Leith Docks on 23 February 1981. These pipes are coated at Leith and railed to various English destinations.

Below left:
Grain from East Anglia is unloaded from a Polybulk bogie hopper wagon at Salkeld Street depot, Glasgow on 26 October 1982. Vans of export traffic on the left include one destined for Geneva. *Mike Macdonald*

Above right:
A potential customer is attracted by the '125 Journey Shrinker' advertising, and by the product itself!

Right:
Open days always bring in the crowds. Over 6,000 came to the Ayr railfayre in October 1983 and saw much to interest them!

12
ScotRail Steam

The success of the West Highland steam operation is the culmination of quite a lot of activity using steam locomotives in Scotland over several years. Generally, appetites for main line steam have been satisfied by the occasional charter train. Among its main line routes Scotland has several that offer challenges to the locomotives amid splendid scenery, so the scene is set for each tour to be a memorable occasion. The line between Stirling and Perth, for example, includes the climbs in both directions to Blackford and Gleneagles. That from Edinburgh to Aberdeen, Britain's longest authorised steam route, crosses the Forth and Tay bridges as well as the difficult sections through Fife and around the Grampian coast.

For some years the major problem was lack of variety of traction. Between 1977 and the end of that decade only 'A4' No 60009 *Union of South Africa* was accessible in Scotland for steam tours. This machine, privately-owned by farmer Cameron and housed in Fife, was actually a star performer and capable of good accelerations and excellent hill climbing, to the delight of enthusiasts and sound recordists. Painted in lined-out BR Brunswick green, she brought back many memories.

But her novelty wore off and her ability to attract custom in Scotland waned. At least one tour was cancelled through lack of support. Then the availability of the Strathspey Railway's 'Black 5' 4-6-0 No 5025 rekindled interest and added the Highland main line to the list of authorised routes.

Meanwhile the Scottish Railway Preservation Society (SRPS) had restored its large LNER 4-4-0, No 246 *Morayshire*, to working order. Her inaugural tour to Dundee in 1980 was restricted by the load she could pull, and was held back by the inadequacy of the watering arrangements. But the SRPS pulled out its trump card with the return to traffic of the novogenarian North British 0-6-0 No 673, named *Maude* after the general, not a lady! As a pair, *Maude* and *Morayshire* could handle a full-length train, and in 1981 they were rostered for a day to the Pullman train run by the Steam Locomotive Operators Association (SLOA) on a long weekend tour from England. The pair covered a route from Larbert through Falkirk to Edinburgh, and later via Shotts to Motherwell.

In 1983 the idea of through specials from England caught on further. One weekend No 60009 covered a roster from Mossend, where she took the train over from an electric locomotive, to Perth and back to Edinburgh, followed another weekend by No 4472 *Flying Scotsman* which was already in Scotland for promotional purposes. *Maude* also took a five-coach special from Falkirk to Perth, but its running was beset by problems, and speed and timekeeping suffered.

N. 673 B.

Then came the Ayr open days in October 1983. *Duchess of Hamilton* and *Maude* were displayed there. No 4472 worked a special there over the Glasgow & South Western route from Annan a week earlier, and No 60009 brought a special from Edinburgh on the first day. It returned with another on the second day and was exhibited there in between.

However, it is clear that a disproportionate amount of administrative time goes into running one-off specials like these – regular, timetabled service (such as the Cumbrian expresses) is less demanding in relation to the revenue earned. Such is the West Highland venture which started as timetabled steam trains on the Mallaig extension in the May 1984 timetable.

For the Fort William-Mallaig trains it was intended to use two ex-LMSR Class 5s. At first only one, No 5407 from Carnforth, was available, and the 0-6-0 *Maude* was despatched to Fort William as reserve engine.

At the May bank holiday weekend, SLOA ran a long-weekend special from England to Fort William, and two connecting trains were laid on from there to Mallaig. These had to run in addition to BR's public steam service on the Monday. No 5407 took the first SLOA train for a return trip to Mallaig, and *Maude* had charge of the second. No 5407 had to make a second return trip with the scheduled service later in the day. Unfortunately, No 673's performance was again lacking in sparkle and at one time services on the extension were almost at a standstill while two steam trains and two diesel-hauled services battled it out for the passing loops. The delays were counter-balanced by the gloriously clear and warm weather on that day, in which the superb scenery of the route shone out at every turn.

The steam venture ran well thence throughout the summer. No 5407 was joined by a second Class 5, No 4767 *George Stephenson*. The West Highland route takings recorded a 43% increase over the previous summer: steam had a significant part to play in that achievement, and is now a regular feature of the ScotRail timetable.

A further venture by BR that was set up at rather short notice was the 'Festival Express' which ran out of Edinburgh across the Forth during the period of the Edinburgh festival. Motive power was short for this and not all trains ran. The 'A4' was one of the engines used on this service.

What is steam's future in Scotland? The two SRPS engines are somewhat smaller than the norm for economic train length running, and will probably play a rare role. Otherwise there is a paucity of steam locomotives in Scotland able to work main line trains. Even the great *Union of South Africa* at the time of writing is awaiting expensive repair work.

Other locomotives, certainly, will be brought in to change the variety on the West Highland line from year to year. The 'K1' and 'K4' 2-6-0s have been quoted as eminently suitable reincarnations from the West Highland line's former days. Apart from the occasional excursion from south of the border, it seems likely therefore that most activity will centre on the Mallaig extension. No-one will seriously regret that.

Table 4
Steam Locomotives Used on Scottish Region 1977-84

Class	Type	Origin	Loco No	Name
A4	4-6-2	LNER	60009	*Union of South Africa*
A3	4-6-2	LNER	4472	*Flying Scotsman*
8P	4-6-0	LMSR	46229*	*Duchess of Hamilton*
5	4-6-0	LMSR	4767#	*George Stephenson*
5	4-6-0	LMSR	5407#	–
5	4-6-0	LMSR	5025‡	–
D49	4-4-0	LNER	246†	*Morayshire*
J36	0-6-0	NBR	673†#	*Maude*

Notes:
* Steamed for Ayr depot open days visit only.
# Used on Mallaig extension, 1984 season.
‡ Kept on Strathspey Railway.
† Kept by Scottish Railway Preservation Society at Falkirk.

Left:
No 673 rests at Motherwell depot after the railtour on 10 May 1981.

Above right:
No 60009 *Union of South Africa* climbs with vigour out of Leuchars on Easter Saturday 1979 with a special from Edinburgh to Aberdeen.

Right:
A feature of No 60009's operations in Scotland is its splendid performance! It is seen here powering away from Hilton Junction, Perth, on 8 October 1977 with an excursion sponsored by Pentlands Round Table.

Left:
On 7 September 1980 the preserved LNER 'D49' 4-4-0 No 246 worked an excursion from Falkirk to Dundee and Perth. *Morayshire* was photographed accelerating away from Ladybank. *Peter J. C. Skelton*

Below left:
What a beautiful pair! North British Railway 0-6-0 No 673 *Maude* pilots LNER 4-4-0 No 246 *Morayshire* across Larbert viaduct on 10 May 1981 on a Steam Locomotive Operators Association special.

Right:
Maude struggles past Blackford on 15 October 1983 with a tour from Falkirk to Perth.

Below:
No 4472 *Flying Scotsman* spent a few weeks in Scotland in October 1983. On the 2nd of that month it is seen approaching Bridge of Earn, between Perth and Ladybank, with a SLOA special.

Left:
The Strathspey Railway's Class 5 4-6-0 No 5025 drew crowds at Glasgow works open day in 1981. It worked a shuttle service to Garnqueen to celebrate 125 years of St Rollox works.

Below left:
No 246 *Morayshire* worked a special train from Craigentinny depot to Rosyth for the Railway Division of the Institution of Mechanical Engineers on 11 May 1983.

Right:
LMS Class 5 No 5407 heads its second train of the day away from Beasdale on the magnificent Fort William to Mallaig route on 27 May 1984. *Peter J. C. Skelton*

Below:
On the same day, No 673 passes the remote chapel near Locheilside, en route from Fort William to Mallaig. *Peter J. C. Skelton*

13
Night Sleeper

It is late evening. Our tourists are replete after the splendid dinner they have enjoyed as their holiday nears its close. On the station concourse, despite the late hour, there is quiet bustle: a passenger train has arrived from the south. Parcels, mails and the first editions of Scottish newspapers are being loaded into a train of parcels vans, bound for England. The night sleeper for London stretches alongside a main platform. Attendants stand by alternate pairs of doors to welcome intending passengers.

'Your ticket, Sir? Reservation? Fine – you'll find Nos 9 and 10 near the middle of the coach. I'll come and see you settled in a few minutes.' Even as they walk along the long corridor the ambience is quietly cushioned. The bright lighting conveys something of the atmosphere of a modern hotel.

The compartment is small but cosy. There is room for luggage under the lower berth and on the rack over the window. The air-conditioning hisses gently to itself through louvres above the door, and the sounds of the outside world are already gone. There is a tap at the door: 'Tea or coffee in the morning, Sir? What time would you want to be called? You don't have to be off the train until 7.30.' The attendant explains the simple individual compartment temperature control, the way the main light can be dimmed, the berth lights and the small blue night light. 'You'll find the washbasin under that shelf, Sir. Is there anything else you want tonight – a drink, perhaps?'

The door closes. They even provide a disposable paper footmat! And impregnated shoe-shine strips! What a good idea to cover the wall next to the berths with a velvet fabric. It is so much warmer to the touch than the usual plastic finish.

The sheets feel crisp, the mattress firm, the blankets light but warm. It is good to relax with a magazine and reflect on the last week or so. Yes, it has been a good holiday. The Scots treated us very well as visitors. The country is so big, so superbly beautiful, and we haven't seen the half of it.

How long have we been moving? I didn't notice us start off! Yes, this is the life. It's certainly better than flying. Next time we've business in Scotland . . .

While the tourists, businessmen, public figures and the not-so-public sleep the miles away, their train is no lone object with the railway to itself at night. The tracks across the border are almost as busy as in the daytime. Sleeper trains are heading south from Aberdeen, Inverness, Edinburgh, Glasgow, Fort William and Stranraer. Some carry normal seating vehicles with their lights sheathed to quieten the glare, and those travellers who can stay awake may be watching films on video screens. The InterCity Sleeper trains share tracks with a succession of heavy Freightliner container trains, timed at 75mph, only 5mph slower than the

Below:
A sleeping car train has the 'right
away' from Dundee in December
1981.

105

sleepers; the fastest things on rails at this hour are the newspaper and postal trains. All of this is prime traffic, bound by the urgency of their contents to meet demanding schedules. And of all of this our travelling tourists are blissfully unaware as they sleep the night through . . .

The tap at the door is firm and sharp. 'It's ten to seven, Sir! Your coffee. Mind you don't knock the tray off the shelf!' Where are we? 'London, Sir, and it's a nice day!' Our tourists drink down the essential coffee, surprised at how fresh they feel. Yesterday evening they dined in Scotland: this morning, breakfast in London. ScotRail was good, and so is InterCity Sleeper!

Table 5
Sleeping Car Services, Scotland – Summer 1985

Time	From	To	via	Distance (miles)
NORTHBOUND				
23.30†	Euston	Glasgow C	WCML	401
23.00	Euston	Glasgow C	GSW	415
21.10	Euston	Stranraer H	GSW	465
21.00	Euston	Inverness	WCML	575
22.40*	Euston	Inverness	WCML	575
21.00	Euston	Fort William	WCML	524
23.35*	King's Cross	Edinburgh	ECML	394
22.15	King's Cross	Aberdeen	ECML	524
20.25	King's Cross	Aberdeen	ECML	524
21.24	Bristol	Glasgow C	WCML	389
21.24	Bristol	Aberdeen	WCML	518
23.30	Glasgow QS	Inverness	Perth	181
23.25	Edinburgh	Inverness	Perth	189
SOUTHBOUND				
23.05†	Glasgow C	Euston	WCML	401
22.15	Glasgow C	Euston	GSW	415
22.00	Stanraer H	Euston	GSW	465
19.30	Inverness	Euston	WCML	575
20.30*	Inverness	Euston	WCML	575
17.40	Fort William	Euston	WCML	524
23.35*	Edinburgh	King's Cross	ECML	394
22.35	Edinburgh	King's Cross	ECML	394
22.00	Aberdeen	King's Cross	ECML	524
20.35	Aberdeen	King's Cross	ECML	524
23.45	Glasgow C	Bristol	WCML	389
20.20	Aberdeen	Bristol	WCML	518
23.30	Inverness	Glasgow QS	Stirling	181
23.30	Inverness	Edinburgh	Stirling	189

Note
* These trains are all-sleeping car trains. Those not so marked convey seated passengers also.
† These trains also carry 'Nightrider' seating vehicles to/from Edinburgh via Carstairs.

Above:
No 47.610 has charge of 14 coaches on the 20.30 from Inverness to London Euston. It was photographed near Carrbridge on 18 July 1984.
Mrs Mary Boocock

Right:
After arrival at Edinburgh on 18 October 1983, the sleepers from Bristol await removal to Craigentinny depot for servicing, bed-making and maintenance.

Below right:
A flashback to the days of the older Mk 1s: No 47.480 leaves Glasgow Central with the empty stock from the previous night's 23.30 from Euston, en route to Polmadie depot on 12 September 1982.

Left:
Train heating vehicle No 97.252 *ETHEL 3* has complemented No 37.085 on the journey from Fort William to Glasgow Queen Street terminus on 20 October 1983. From here, the sleeping cars will be tripped to link up with an Inverness-Euston train.

Above:
History is in the making at Glasgow Queen Street. The Mk 1 sleeping car No W2423 is on the 23.30 to Inverness on the last night when Mk 1 sleeping cars operated in BR public service, 13 May 1984.

Right:
No 27.012 has the Inverness sleeping car at the head of empty stock being dragged up the 1 in 40 from Glasgow Queen Street, bound for Cowlairs depot on 22 March 1983.

Appendix 1

Locomotive Depot Allocations, 20 January 1986

Eastfield (Glasgow) – ED (total 116)
47.004/006/108/117/120/157/206/209/469/470/562/578/593/595/
   617/636/640/641/644

37.011/012/014/022/026/027/033/034/041/043/051/056/081/085/
   108/111/112/117/125/133/151/175/178/191/292/401-413/
   422-424

27.001/008/014/024/030/038/041/045/046/056/059/063/066/204/
   206-208

20.048/063/067/095/100/102/100/114/126/127/137/145/154/156/
   171/175/179/181/184/189/191-193/198/199/201/202/213/216/
   217/228

08.720/738/793/851-853/938/952

Haymarket (Edinburgh) – HA (total 109)
47.001/003/012/017/018/040/049/053/109/118/210/269/274/430/
   492/630/701-716

27.004/010/012/017/018/020/023/033/036/037/040/051-055

26.001-008/010/011/014/015/021/023/024/027-029/034/037/039/
   040-042/046

20.203-206/208/211/212/218-227

08.421/570/571/710/718/726/755/763/881

Inverness – IS (total 52)
47.460/461/464/467/517/541/546/550/586/604/614/653

37.021/025/035/114/183/260-264/414-421

27.003/005/025/026/042/047-050/064/065

26.025/026/031/032/035/036/038/043

08.621/717/754

Motherwell – ML (total 30)
37.018/030/037/049/088/099/137/145/146/152/155-157/184/188/
   190/192

20.122-124/138

08.430*/561/565/581/730/731/733/736/883
   * Vacuum braked only, retained for NCB use

Shields (Glasgow) – GW (total 18)
81.002-014/017/019-022

Thornton – TJ (total 8)
08.515/712/732/753/761/762/764/827

Ayr – AY (total 7)
08.448/449/591/693/727/735/855

Ferryhill (Aberdeen) – AB (total 3)
08.680/791/882

Grangemouth – GM (total 3)
08.620/630/725

Appendix 2

Named ScotRail Locomotives, 20 January 1986

37.012 *Loch Rannoch*
37.026 *Loch Awe*
37.027 *Loch Eil*
37.043 *Loch Lomond*
37.081 *Loch Long*
37.111 *Outward Bound – Loch Eil*
37.114 *Dunrobin Castle*
37.188 *Jimmy Shand*
37.260 *Radio Highland*
37.261 *Caithness*
37.262 *Dounreay*
37.401 *Mary Queen of Scots*
37.402 *Oor Wullie*
37.403 *Isle of Mull*
37.404 *Ben Cruachan*

47.120 *RAF Kinloss*
47.461 *Charles Rennie Mackintosh*
47.469 *Glasgow Chamber of Commerce*
47.470 *University of Edinburgh*
47.517 *Andrew Carnegie*
47.541 *The Queen Mother*
47.546 *Aviemore Centre*
47.550 *University of Dundee*
47.562 *Sir William Burrell*
47.578 *The Royal Society of Edinburgh*
47.593 *Galloway Princess*
47.595 *Confederation of British Industry*
47.617 *University of Stirling*

47.701 *Saint Andrew*
47.702 *Saint Cuthbert*
47.703 *Saint Mungo*
47.704 *Dunedin*
47.705 *Lothian*
47.706 *Strathclyde*
47.707 *Holyrood*
47.708 *Waverley*
47.709 *The Lord Provost*
47.710 *Sir Walter Scott*
47.711 *Greyfriars Bobby*
47.712 *Lady Diana Spencer*
47.713 *Tayside Region*
47.714 *Grampian Region*
47.716 *Duke of Edinburgh Award*

43088 *XIII Commonwealth Games 1986*
43091 *Edinburgh Military Tattoo*
43092 *Highland Chieftain*
43100 *Craigentinny*
43101 *Edinburgh International Festival*

Other Named Vehicles

Train electric heat vehicles

97.250 *ETHEL 1*
97.251 *ETHEL 2*
97.252 *ETHEL 3*

Appendix 3

ScotRail Facts and Figures

Rail Passenger

	1980	1981	1982	1983	1984
Receipts (£m)	81.4	87.9	76.4	91.6	91.7
Journeys made ('000s)	61.5	57.9	49.5	55.7	52.0
Trains run daily:					
Loco-hauled	268	256	256	230	235
DMU	544	550	520	532	535
EMU	797	797	797	774	774
Punctuality (within 5 mins):					
InterCity Anglo-Scottish	62%	72%	70%	63%	65%
ScotRail, loco-hauled	73%	83%	74%	81%	82%
ScotRail, DMU	83%	88%	86%	90%	91%
ScotRail, EMU	90%	91%	94%	96%	96%
Number of stations:					
staffed	255	249	246	233	230
unstaffed	35	41	44	50	57
opened	–	–	–	–	4
closed	–	–	–	7	–

Railfreight

	1980	1981	1982	1983	1984
Receipts (£m)	34.3	40.4	34.8	33.1	23.7
Freight forwarded:					
Coal (million tonnes)	6.0	6.0	5.1	4.0	1.0
Metals	2.6	3.9	3.1	3.3	2.4
Other traffics	3.0	2.3	2.2	2.0	2.0
Freight received (all)	12.8	13.1	11.1	10.1	6.5
Train miles ('000s):					
Speedlink	670	690	1,154	2,097	2,151
Freightliner	1,280	1,150	1,013	1,202	1.005
Merry-go-round	290	330	199	93	96
Company trains	2,090	1,620	1,709	1,642	1,618
Vacuum network	3,970	3,220	2,337	507	159

Rail Express Parcels

	1980	1981	1982	1983	1984
Receipts (£m)	6.0	4.6	3.4	3.5	3.5
Train run daily	49	38	36	41	41
Number of stations	151	141	139	105	101

Personnel

	1980	1981	1982	1983	1984
Wages staff	13,962	13,346	12,830	12,418	12,076
Salaried staff	4,665	4,551	4,169	4,075	3,775
Total staff	18,627	17,897	16,999	16,493	15,851

Track and Signalling

	1980	1981	1982	1983	1984
Track:					
Route miles	1,800	1,790	1,782	1,743	1,705
Track miles	2,882	2,838	2,810	2,790	2,620
Electrified route miles	232	239	239	239	241
Electrified track miles	538	548	548	548	556
Signal boxes	232	207	201	193	177
Power boxes	16	16	19	19	20
Bridges	9,500	9,420	9,260	9,220	9,210
Tunnels	83	83	83	83	83

Busiest, Longest and Biggest

Busiest stations (receipts):
- Edinburgh (£12m)
- Glasgow C (£11m)
- Aberdeen (£6m)
- Glasgow QS (£6m)
- Dundee (£3m)

Busiest freight terminals (tonnes handled):
- Leith South (55,584)
- Aberdeen (27,161)
- Gl Salkeld St (21,343)
- Falkirk (15,804)
- Dundee (11,832)

Longest bridge: Tay bridge (2,967m)
Longest viaduct: Ratho, Bathgate (665m)
Longest tunnel: Newton Street, Greenock (1,930m)
Longest platform: Edinburgh (10/11) (496m)

Late News

Scotrail has moved on in many ways since the main text for this book was prepared and updated!

To launch the conversion of the Glasgow-Aberdeen service to push-pull working in May 1985, the whole group of push-pull trains running between Edinburgh, Glasgow and Aberdeen was relaunched under the brand name 'ScotRail Express'. All the locomotives ('47/7s') and stock (Mk 2 and 3a air-conditioned) were repainted in ScotRail livery. The trains were advertised as being for 100mph running and a new 'ScotRail Express' symbol applied to the coaches and on publicity material. Public awareness of the services has improved, and the carryings are said to be up.

A new sleeping car service from Glasgow Queen Street to Aberdeen was launched on 30 September 1985. It uses spare Mk 3a vehicles attached to the 23.30 from Glasgow to Inverness as far as Perth, and completes what has long-felt been a missing link in the Scottish internal overnight trains.

New stations were opened in 1985 at Porthleven, between Aberdeen and Stonehaven; Livingstone on the Edinburgh-Shotts line; and Bridge of Allan between Stirling and Dunblane. Results from the reopened station at Dyce, northwest of Aberdeen, are becoming most encouraging.

Catering trolly service has become a permanent feature on Edinburgh-Glasgow push-pull trains which carry no catering car as such. The idea was originally initiated by Travellers Fare train staff, and has proved to be a viable operation. A private enterprise operator provides a trolley service on certain trains on the Stranraer-Carlisle route. A novel idea is a Travellers Fare trolley at breakfast time on a morning EMU commuter 'fast' train from Helensburgh to Glasgow!

Resignalling at Dundee in 1985 has been accompanied by track rationalisation and re-alignment of the main lines west of the station there. Now trains from Glasgow and Edinburgh have a straighter approach, but the semaphore signals (see picture on page 48) have gone.

ScotRail has announced plans to make significant improvements at every station in the Region, to smarten the railway's image in all localities. The Regional Civil Engineer has been allocated a specific budget to ensure that the improved appearances are then maintained in the years to come.

Special liveries were applied in 1985 to tourist trains on the West Highland lines. The Mk1 set used for the steam trains is now in former LNER 'tourist' green and cream livery. A two-car double power-car Class 104 DMU has been put in service on a summer diagram between Oban and Crianlarich, which permits connections with Glasgow-Fort William trains. The unit is painted a startling yellow and maroon style, thus gaining the nickname 'Mexican bean'.

A project is under consideration to link the far north route near Georgemas Junction direct with a new nuclear waste plant being proposed for Dounreay. This could provide traffic which would be a positive step to securing the route's long term future.

The use of ETHELs to heat trains in motion is drawing to a close. The first '37/4s' equipped with electric train supply alternators were delivered from Crewe works in the summer of 1985 and put to work on the West Highland lines. Steam heating in Scotland is expected to be eliminated in May 1986, with the allocation of '37/4s' to Inverness for the far north services. No 37.401 has been named *Mary Queen of Scots*.

Below:
Class 47 No 47.716 *Duke of Edinburgh Award* was one of four '47/4s' converted in 1985 to push-pull operation at Crewe Works for the inauguration of the Glasgow-Aberdeen 'ScotRail Express' service in May. It is seen at Queen Street station at the head of the 09.25 to Aberdeen on 20 September 1985.

Index